Hindsight to Foresight

LEARN FROM TRENDS & EXPERIENCES

ANKUSH AHUJA

ISBN 979-8-89544-875-5

"It's a bit counter-intuitive to think about the future in terms of the past. But...I've learned an important trick: to develop foresight, you need to practice hindsight. Technologies, cultures, and climates may change, but our basic human needs and desires - to survive, to care for our families, and to lead happy, purposeful lives - remain the same."

— Jane McGonigal

Contents

Contents

Introduction

A s we experience more of life's glories and gain wisdom across our personal and professional journey, we often wonder, "what if I understood this before" or "why didn't I know myself early in my life as I know now"?

Though I am convinced that my life could have been better if there was a way to connect the dots forward, but we all know that's not the way life works. I often wonder a possibility of sharing the role hindsight plays in life and how to recognise it from time to time.

There are seeds of potential growth and improvement embedded in our past experiences. We can find those promising seeds in our successes as well as in our failures. But we must be willing to take the time and effort to look back and ask questions.

But what's more important than the specific questions is how you ask them — the attitude and mindset you bring to the task.

Hindsight questioning is only worth doing if you do it with a positive, productive, and forward-looking frame of mind. One of the pitfalls of engaging in hindsight is that you can become mired in regret: If only I'd done X or Y, instead of what I actually did at the time. Or, if I'd known then what I know now, what would I have done differently?

But there's no point speculating about the past. It's important to resolve, at the outset, that you're going to ask hindsight questions designed to extract learning and insights that can be applied in the present or future.

What types of questions should you ask? Start with diagnostic ones. Looking at past actions or events, ask: *What worked? What didn't work?*

To move to a deeper level of diagnostic inquiry, ask "why" questions, as in, *Why did I choose that particular approach or strategy? Why did I feel confident, at the time, that I was doing the right thing?*

This book is a result of series of experiential learnings that I started documenting in the form of letters to my son, in the process, it seemed worthwhile sharing more broadly. I have captured key learnings that are commonly heard of but understood much later in life and often brings regret.

Is there a need of another self-help book when there are millions available for any subject you can imagine, maybe not. Therefore, this book is intended to be a relatable journey to reflect on the life and hopefully recognise commonality without prejudice and not be disheartened by some experiences.

Before we start...

Before I go into the things I wish I'd known earlier, I want to just briefly touch on the process of acquiring wisdom because interestingly, although part of me says, *"Gee, I wish I'd known that 20 years ago"*, it really is a moot point.

I often wonder, if I'd known something 20 years ago, would I have been mature enough to put it into action? Would I have had the capacity to understand it the way I do now? Would I have even recognized its importance?

Okay, so I've gone deep early, but this is an important point about the process, and it's our first principle: When the student is ready, the teacher appears.

Where you are at any point in your life makes a difference to what you are able to learn and absorb. So, for example, try re-reading one of your favourite books, which you haven't read in a while. You'll see completely different things than you did the first-time round. That's because it isn't just about the words on the page. A book is a dialogue between the author and the reader. When different readers open that first page, they're starting at a completely different point.

As the famous saying goes:

No two persons read the same book……Edmund Wilson

In the hands of one reader, a book may be completely uninspiring and dull. In another reader's hands, that same book will *completely transform* the way they view the world.

The second principle about the learning process is that all of the lessons are cumulative. As you build your path through your career and life, the choices you make set you up for the next set of choices.

When I made the choice to leave my well settled career in India to migrate to Australia without a job or an even an idea or a strategy to get a job, I didn't know whether it was the right decision. It was the toughest one to make. I knew it was an *expensive* decision with many unknowns like:

What if I do not like to live in a foreign land?

What if I never find a satisfying job?

Will I ever be able to catch up on the career I left to start afresh?

But now, as I look back, I know exactly why and how I made that choice. It opened up the path to what I do now. A different decision 10 years ago would've taken me down a completely different road, even though I didn't realize it at the time.

But just take a moment to reflect on this at the micro level. Deciding to do something difficult today will have a huge impact on tomorrow, because when the same choice arises tomorrow, you'll either feel *more* confident or *less* confident about it, based on what you chose to do yesterday.

As you build greater resilience and more experience, you also build your capacity to go to the next level. Think of it like a video game. You have to complete the level you're on before you get to progress to the next level. If you were just parachuted into level 42 all of a sudden, you wouldn't know how or why you were there, and you wouldn't last very long. Whatever knowledge got you to that level would be perishable.

Chapter 1

Insight on Hindsight

It is a raining winter Saturday in Sydney; Australia and it's been almost 4 continuous gloomy days, and I am terrible missing sunshine. Growing up in New Delhi, India, my favourite season has always been winters, however that changed about ten years back when I moved to Sydney permanently. This city is to be lived to its full glory in summer when the sun is out till late and there are activities galore and the countless beaches buzzing with excitement and activities.

As I finish my extra hot latte and settle down in my home office hoping for the dreadful rain to end, it suddenly dawns on me that its almost 5 pm and I am supposed to join my lovely wife at our friend's place for dinner and drinks. I quickly get ready and decide to take an uber in case I have a few drinks, it's always a good idea to keep that option open.

I order an uber and within 3 minutes, a clean uber green is on my doorstep and we are ready to commence our 19 minutes journey. Although, we are used to this level of comfort of service for years now, I remember vividly when taking a taxi was a cumbersome and time-consuming experience. Travis Kalanick, the founder of uber as per me is one of the geniuses of our times to have imagined a travel experience using first principles thinking and not just iterating on existing taxi experience.

Suddenly, I realise that before giving 100% credit of reimagining the travel experience successfully to Travis Kalanick and the founding team, it's worthwhile pondering over the importance of incremental innovations of the past.

If we need to study or appreciate the true origins of a seamless travel experience on demand, we need to go back and appreciate the importance of the following incremental breakthrough innovations namely:

1. Smart phones

2. GPS

3. Internet on the go

4. Mobile app infrastructure

5. Maps

6. Credit card payment on the go.

Though all the above innovations are truly significant on their own but it's easy to miss the incremental advantage of these leading to a so-called disruptive technology which changes people's experiences fundamentally until that becomes a norm and a minimum standard and expectation. The breakthrough of a modern smart phone has its foundations in the seemingly insignificant innovations like a touchscreen, mobile application infrastructure and the list goes on.

Roger Lee Easton. Sr – the true inventor of Global Positioning System known as GPS might never have imagined that his invention will be one of the foundational stones for modern life.

But is uber truly a disruptive innovation on its own? Now that's not an easy debate to win, is it? However, its undisputable that each breakthrough innovation has parents, grandparents, great grandparents, siblings, or cousins leading to the building blocks of the grand innovation. The same is true for any major breakthrough which not that long ago would have seemed an impossibility like a space rocket which regularly transports humans and payload to space centre like an ordinary mode of transport.

Isn't this why it's often said that "hindsight is notably cleverer than foresight". We all understand the value and power of understanding a situation or an event after it has happened but still why is it common to ignore the power of hindsight?

Let's use our power of hindsight to reflect on significant atrocities humans have witnessed like world wars. It's easy for us to say that the war was wrong, but we have the advantage and a benefit of hindsight.

In hindsight, it's clear that there were alternatives. Can we use our hindsight to create a better foresight?

Let me bring you attention to another valuable hindsight which also related to the power of storytelling – more on storytelling in later chapter though. I am not sure if you have read about or seen stories of an unsinkable ship named "Lusitania"? Perhaps nothing symbolized the power of human ingenuity more than ocean liners like the Lusitania also referred as an unsinkable ship in 1915. With her solid steam powered engine and record speed. The Lusitania could cross the ocean in mere days, just few decades earlier, such a journey could have taken months. It was a luxurious engineering marvel of the time captained by the famous William Turner.

Compelled to save money, Captain William Turner shut down the fourth boiler room on his giant steamship for its passage from New York to Liverpool. The decision would slow the ship's voyage by one day—an annoyance, but worth the savings as the passenger-ship industry struggled economically.

Little did he or anyone else know how fateful the decision would be.

The delay meant Turner's ship—the Lusitania—would now sail directly into the path of a German submarine.

The Lusitania was hit with a torpedo, killing nearly twelve hundred passengers, and becoming the most important trigger to rally U.S. public support for entering World War I.

Had the fourth boiler room been operating, Turner would have reached Liverpool a day before the German submarine had even entered the Celtic Sea, where it crossed paths with the Lusitania. The ship likely would have avoided an attack. A country may have avoided a war that became the seed event for the rest of the twentieth century.

Since, we are on the topic of war, it is reasonable to infer that women participation in workforce was encourage somewhere in the middle of World War 2. Most of the available fit men were encouraged to help war efforts in some shape or form and factories were struggling without required labour in an era where more production was needed. This also led to efforts in creating efficient and less manual efforts in factories and these efficiencies led to significant small innovations like machines which had incremental impact in factories.

Post World War 2, the world had seen damage and loss that could never have been predicted at the time. People's sentiments were at its lowest and general trust in leaders and government was almost non-existent. This led to an idea of guaranteed benefits by the establishment which we now commonly refer as Social Security.

Does guaranteed social security disincentivises people to look for meaningful work?

It's astonishing to believe that the World War 2 started on horses in 1931 and ended with the most sophisticated nuclear bombs.

Does uncertainty and instability lead to faster innovation?

Do people achieve unachievable outcomes faced with adversity or loss of life?

Pondering over these counter intuitive thoughts is only possible through hindsight and that is precisely the reason why hindsight is so powerful.

Chapter 2

Bill Gates and the World of Computers

Who is responsible for the birth of "Microsoft", is it Bill Gates or Bill Dougall?

Is Bill Gates a true genius or just plain lucky?

I do not wish you to blame your ignorance for not knowing who Bill Dougall was or the direct role he played in founding the organisation which truly changed the world. Bill Dougall was a World War II navy pilot turned high school math and science teacher. "He believed that book study wasn't enough without real-world experience. He also realized that we'd need to know something about computers when we got to college," recalled late Microsoft co-founder Paul Allen. This is a classic example of foresight concluded with the benefit of "hindsight".

The story of how Lakeside School, just outside Seattle, even got a computer is remarkable.

In 1968 Dougall petitioned the Lakeside School Mothers' Club to use the proceeds from its annual rummage sale — about $3,000 — to lease a Teletype Model 30 computer hooked up to the General Electric mainframe terminal for computer time-sharing. "The whole idea of time-sharing only got invented in 1965," Gates later said. "Someone was pretty forward-looking." Most university graduate schools did not have a computer anywhere near as advanced as Bill Gates had access to in eighth grade. And he couldn't get enough of it.

Bill Gates was 13 years old in 1968 when he met classmate Paul Allen. Allen was also obsessed with the school's computer, and the two hit it off.

Lakeside's computer wasn't part of its general curriculum. It was an independent study program. Bill and Paul could toy away with the thing at their leisure, letting their creativity run wild — after school, late into the night, on weekends. They quickly became computing experts.

During one of their late-night sessions, Allen recalled Gates showing him a Fortune magazine and saying, "What do you think it's like to run a Fortune 500 company?" Allen said he had no idea. "Maybe we'll have our own computer company someday," Gates said. Microsoft is now worth more than a trillion dollars.

A little quick math.

In 1968 there were roughly 303 million high-school-age people in the world, according to the UN.

About 18 million of them lived in the United States.

About 270,000 of them lived in Washington state.

A little over 100,000 of them lived in the Seattle area.

And only about 300 of them attended Lakeside School.

Start with 303 million, end with 300.

One in a million high-school-age students attended the high school that had the combination of cash and foresight to buy a computer.

Bill Gates happened to be one of them.

Gates is not shy about what this meant. "If there had been no Lakeside, there would have been no Microsoft," he told the school's graduating class in 2005.

Gates is staggeringly smart, even more hardworking, and as a teenager had a vision for computers that even most seasoned computer executives couldn't grasp. He also had a one in a million head start by going to school at Lakeside.

Now let me tell you about Gates' friend Kent Evans. He experienced an equally powerful dose of luck's close sibling, risk.

Bill Gates and Paul Allen became household names thanks to Microsoft's success. But back at Lakeside, there was a third member of this gang of high-school computer prodigies.

Kent Evans and Bill Gates became best friends in eighth grade. Evans was, by Gates' own account, the best student in the class.

The two talked "on the phone ridiculous amounts," Gates recalls in the documentary Inside Bill's Brain. "I still know Kent's phone number," he says. "525–7851."

Evans was as skilled with computers as Gates and Allen. Lakeside once struggled to manually put together the school's class schedule — a maze of complexity to get hundreds of students the classes they need at times that don't conflict with other courses. The school tasked Bill and Kent — children, by any measure — to build a computer program to solve the problem. It worked.

And unlike Paul Allen, Kent shared Bill's business mind and endless ambition. "Kent always had the big briefcase, like a lawyer's briefcase," Gates recalls. "We were always scheming about what we'd be doing five or six years in the future. Should we go be CEOs? What kind of impact could you have? Should we go be generals? Should we go be ambassadors?" Whatever it was, Bill and Kent knew they'd do it together.

After reminiscing on his friendship with Kent, Gates trails off.

"We would have kept working together. I'm sure we would have gone to college together." Kent could have been a founding partner of Microsoft with Gates and Allen.

But it would never happen. Kent died in a mountaineering accident before he graduated high school.

Every year there are around three dozen mountaineering deaths in the United States as per government records. The odds of being killed on a mountain in high school are roughly one in a million.

Bill Gates experienced one in a million luck by ending up at Lakeside. Kent Evans experienced one in a million risk by never getting to finish what he and Gates set out to achieve. The same force, the same magnitude, working in opposite directions.

Chapter 3

Stability is De-stabilizing

Australia is one of the most beautiful countries to live in and its prominent cities continuously rank in the best ten cities in the world. One of the peculiar traits of Australians is passion for property and house ownership which is one of the highest in comparable countries. Australians are considered as one of the wealthiest people on average in the world almost totally based on home ownership rates and their continuous appreciation in value – more about that later though.

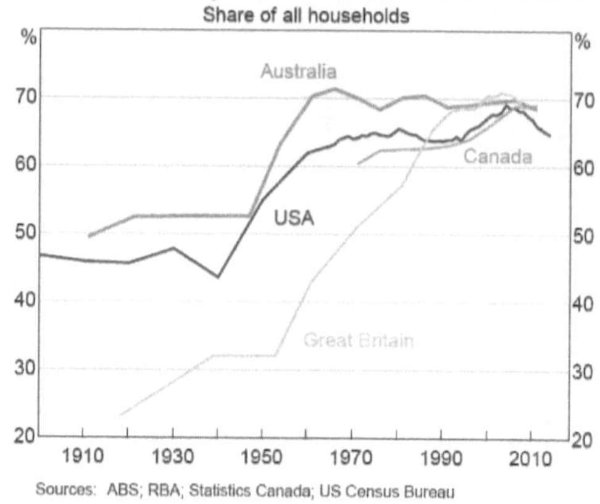

Home Ownership Rates for Selected Countries

Now, guess what the most common topic of conversation in parties, get together and in general – you guessed right, its property market. This topic is closely followed by beer of course. No Wonder an Australian dream is referred as "Owning your own home on your block of land with picked fence".

Over the past 25 years, the median house value in Australia has risen by a staggering 412% as per government records. It is solid to assume that property market down under is as stable as it gets, However, approximately every four to five years the market slows and then recovers – this is generally the period which generates significant stress amongst people. The trends are same as ever but still a sort of panic sets in. This trend most recently was visible post covid.

Now let's look at it closely, when the property market is stable for a long-term outperforming other significant asset class, people tend to invest more. To invest more, householders borrow more, more borrowing in the market usually leads to increase in interest rates or mandated serviceability calculations and a fair bit of interference from central bank to cool it off depending on its presumable impact on inflation of course.

High interest rates or other interventions from central bank leads to strain on household affordability due to high loan repayments leading to reduced activity in the sector. Reduced activity in the market leads to

Falling prices due to mismatch in demand and supply curve until the market corrects itself.

This trend has been consistent in the last few decades and by now householders should start expecting these cycles, but this is far from true. Stability often leads to instability.

Let me illustrate the same argument in the context of financial markets. In the ten years period from 2012 to 2022, stock values have more than doubled.

Stock index values more than doubled since 2012

Data source: S&P Dow Jones, NASDAQ OMX Group

Barring few downturns on regular intervals, stock market has shown significant upwards trends. You would assume that by now investors and intermediaries would be expecting few market corrections along the way, this is far from true. Every short-term downtrend leads to panic selling and windfall gains depending on which way you want to look at.

Imagine if markets continue to be stable and without a downturn, what will happen to the value of stocks? People would be comfortable to sell their homes to invest in the stock market, some might even consider selling their kidney. Market corrects itself leading to disproportionate returns to investors which has always been true.

Minsky Hypothesis

Hyman Minsky was an economist at Washington University in St. Louis from 1965 to 1990. He proposed a theory he labelled the financial instability hypothesis, which holds that the economy creates its own bubbles and crashes. The gist of his theory is that stable economies sow the seeds of their own destruction because stability, seeming safe, encourages people to take risks. That risk-taking creates financial instability that eventually results in panic and crisis.

Unfortunately, during his lifetime, neither Minsky nor his hypothesis was taken seriously. He died in 1996, before the dotcom bubble and the Great Recession, both of which gave credence to his ideas. His theory is now accepted as a primary explanation for the boom-and-bust cycles in the economy.

The financial instability hypothesis is rooted in swings between excessive risk-taking and the panic that follows when the risk-taking overheats and the economy collapses. Increased risk in the economy can be seen in the terms on which debt is incurred. Minsky hypothesized three stages of lending he dubbed hedge, speculative, and Ponzi.

During the hedge stage, lenders and borrowers are cautious because of the losses they incurred in the prior recession. Borrowers are Vary of leverage, and lenders make loans in modest amounts with stringent credit requirements. During this stage, the amount of debt in the system is reasonable.

In the following speculative stage, market participants become more confident of a recovery. Borrowers take on greater amounts of debt, and the economy begins to boom. Lenders grant credit based on ever-lower standards, assuming that asset prices will continue to rise. During this stage, borrowers can cover the interest on the loans, but become less able to repay the principal.

By the final Ponzi stage, lenders and borrowers have forgotten the lessons of the prior crisis. Everyone is sure that asset prices will continue to rise, and debt is granted with repayments based on that assumption. The economy becomes over-leveraged; debt and risk-taking have created a financial house of cards.

Paradoxically, Minsky's hypothesis teaches us that the time of greatest investment risk is when everything seems good, and investing is actually least risky when, as Baron Rothschild once put it, there is "blood in the streets."

Stability is destablising...........................

Chapter 4

Motivation Trap

Motivation often comes after starting, not before.

Over a period of corporate life, I have attended countless meetings, trainings and seminars on "motivation" which led me to believe that its essential for everyone to be motivated at work and life in general. I have encouraged my team to work on identifying what motivates them and worked with them to constantly create individual plans for team members.

For the longest time, I believed that money and growth are the two biggest motivating factors in people's lives. Gradually, I have realized that motivation is an overrated concept. I have been planning to write a book for years but somehow, I kept telling myself that I need to wait for a right motivation to find a subject I am passionate about and a suitable mindset to devote significant time to write.

Until I read a book called "someday is today" by Matthew Dicks, he is one of my favourite storytellers and his books are a treat. In the beginning, he describes an incident "he is sitting in a McDonald restaurant speaking to a woman who wants to become novelist, she asks him for a few minutes of his time, and he agreed. She proposed a local coffee shop, but he does not drink coffee and he tells her to meet at McDonalds instead. They are sitting on stools at the back of the restaurant, she is asking him questions about literary agents, book contracts and international sales, film rights and royalties. He listens carefully and answers all her questions waiting for the right time to ask his own, the question far important then any question she has asked so far. He finally gets an opening and asks, so…how is the book coming?

She says looking a little startled…hmmm…I have not really started yet. He was afraid of his answer and saw it coming from a country mile away. Really why not? He says sounding surprised. She says the writing process is complicated for her, she finds that she can only write for two-to-three-hour increments at a time, and she really needs to be in a right space to work like a quite coffee shop or a park bench mid-morning cappuccino at the ready. She hopes to dedicate a year of her life to writing this book and she wants to understand the publishing world first before beginning. He nods and bites his tongue. So what is you writing process she asks him?

He has lots of answers to this question. He would like to remind her that American soldiers in gas masks were squatting in rains soak trenches in World War 1 scribbling words on pages as bullets and bombs filled the sky over their head. Her need for a coffee shop, a cappuccino heated perfectly at one hundred and fifty-four degrees Celsius with smooth jazz is a joke. But he does not say that he likes to tell her that she does not want to write… she wants to have written.

She is fond of what she imagines the writing life to be like – mid morning visits to the coffee shop to splash a few hundred words on a page before enjoying a late lunch with friends but she is not prepared to do the actual work required to produce something worthy of people's time and money nor she is passionate enough to engage in the craft in those less then ideal moments. Writers cannot help but write, they do not wait to write, they are compelled to write but he does not say this either. He instead says, you were seven minutes late arriving here today, she opens her mouth to apologise but he stops her – no its fine, you have never been here before and that is not my point. Then what is your point she asks? Do you know how I spent those seven minutes he asks. I don't know she said, he says "I wrote nine good sentences".

The above excerpts from chapter 2 titled 86,400 Seconds changed my life and I believe I have conditioned my mind to not wait for any motivation or ideal time to work on something that is meaningful to me. Thank you, Matthew Dicks.

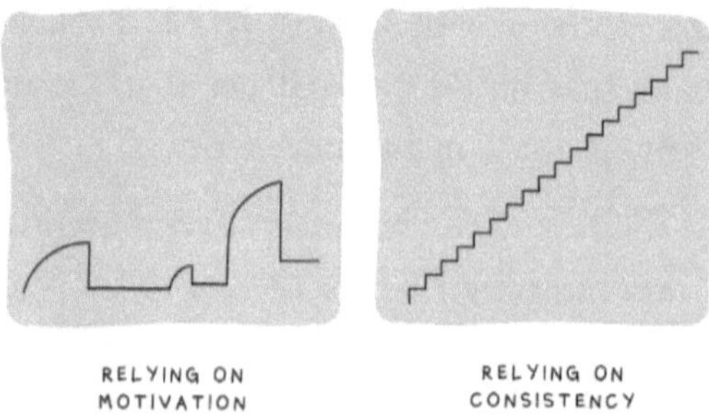

If you rely on motivation in your life, you will become addicted to positive memes and inspirational people/talks to lift your dopamine levels. You will need them like a daily drug to get you going.

And you will get addicted to social media because it fuels this addiction. You will spend your energy chasing instead of doing.

Please don't. You will end up being an easy target for people trying to sell you stuff to keep you pumped.

Chapter 5

Paradox of Optimism

I have had a rare honour and privilege of meeting Eddie Jaku in person in September 2019 at the Sydney Jewish Museum. Eddie Jaku was an holocaust survivor and whose memoir "The Happiest Man on Earth" is a true masterpiece. The audio version of the book is narrated by the man himself and I could truly feel the emotions in his voice. If someone decides to read just one book is his or her lifetime, I recommend "The Happiest Man on Earth" without a hesitation. I have already preserved a copy for my son to read when he reaches a suitable age.

Eddie Jaku moved to Sydney, Australia in 1950 as a stateless refugee and rebuilt his life. After retirement, he devoted to his life to spread awareness about holocaust and his experiences in concentration camps.

As me and my friend Howard enter the Sydney Jewish Museum in Darlinghurst around noon, we see a picture of Eddie Jaku on the noticeboard. He was there to informally speak to the friends and families of Holocaust victims. I am thrilled to see him sitting on wooden chair surrounded by people and having a conversation and answering questions.

Post the session, I gather courage to walk up Eddie and say "yours has been the most inspirational book I have ever read and would love to speak to you for five minutes". Eddie was 99 years young at that time, he smiles and agrees to have a chat with an exciting demeanour. As I finish introducing myself, I confess that I have read and listened to his book numerous times and often go back to specific chapters when I need inspiration. I then continue the discussion and ask him, are there any other valuable insights about life that he would like to share with me?

He thinks about it for a few seconds and talks about optimism in general. He says "when we faced inhuman conditions in Auschwitz, fellow camp members who were optimistic about the war will end anytime now and they will be with their families soon were amongst the first ones to give up hope. As weeks turned into months, their hopes vanished and their bodies gave up, as a part of routine health check-up were declared unfit to work hence made their way to gas chamber or chose to end their lives.

I could not resist myself and ask him another question fully expecting him not to indulge me further but to my astonishment, he was happy to share his learnings and experience.

I ask him, "how did you manage to survive the inhuman conditions and tortures of Auschwitz?"

He said, "the answer is hope", then he continues:

"I promised when I came out of the darkest hours of my life that I would be happy for the rest of my life and smile, because if you smile, the world smiles with you. Life is not always happiness. Sometimes, there are many hard days. But you must remember that you are lucky to be alive — we are all lucky in this way. Every breath is a gift. Life is beautiful if you let it be. Happiness is in your hands."

I will never forget the day I had a rare privilege of meeting Eddie.

Chapter 6

The Pig and the Chicken

I have always been an average student with peculiar interests in certain subjects that were hard to combine in high school. I did exceedingly well in business studies, physics and political science and was disheartened to learn that there is no particular stream available in my school to combine these subjects or even country I grew up in. If you were born in eighties and entered high school in nighties, chances are you would have faced a version of this predicament.

I used to be jealous of my friends who had their subjects sorted out in advance and some of them had a version of their career already decided in their heads. In one of the important seminars organised by my school, the presentation began with introduction of esteemed school alumni, highlighted their curriculum vitae and the success they achieved in professional world. While each alumni had impressive and motivating stories to share, and I acknowledge that each journey was different.

However, one common thread binding all their careers was that each of them were clear on their chosen field of higher studies and the industry or even a role within the industry they wanted to specialise in.

I attended the seminar with the hope of being able to decide my field of studies in high school and hopefully be able to visualise my ultra successful career and eventual retirement with a beach house and a sports car. In reality, I felt like a loser who had no idea or a plan with just two weeks left to finally decide whether its science, commerce or humanities are right choices for me to be a highly successful and sort after professional. This led to numerous questions in my head while the distinguished faculties were busy clicking pictures with their ex-students and basking in the glory and perhaps crediting themselves by exaggerating the role they played shaping these successful lives.

The most anticipated session of this seminar was Q&A with alumni which generated questions like:

How difficult was for you to choose your specialisation?

How is real professional life different from student life?

How can we become as successful as you?

What is the one thing you will like us to focus on?

When the Q&A session was finally over, I reluctantly raise my hand (without realising that I actually did) and to my bad luck, the convener called my name and invited me to ask the question even when the session was over. I started sweating profusely and did not want to give the impression that I don't know what I want to do in my life? I gathered all my courage and asked (no one in particular) but in general the following question.

When you reflect on your school and successful professional life, what is one thing you would change if you had an opportunity all over again?

This question was greeted with stunned silence and none of the esteemed alumni wanted to take a lead, after about sixty seconds (though it was difficult to tell you the exact duration), a successful IT professional said something that led almost everyone in the hall to focus. His exact words (which I can never forget in my life) were:

"Though I am the one of the best IT professionals in my field and earning much more than I ever dreamed, I wish I learned and worked in the sales or product management side of the business."

This sort of an answer though delayed the much-awaited lunch at the end of seminar but led to another successful chemical engineer to admit that he regrets not pursuing mathematics in high school since his father wanted him to become a chemical engineer since he was conceived. Later over lunch, he acknowledged that he often feels fatigued and lack of interest in his current career but it's too late for him since he has family responsibilities.

I decide to follow my gut and opted to specialise in commerce with an additional elective subject of political science. I did extremely well in high school and the choices I made worked well for me. After completing my high school with above average marks and topping my entire school in "business studies", I decided to continue pursuing commerce for my university as well.

Having just completed my graduation while working night shifts to make some money and learn & experience corporate life (not a single person in my family worked in corporate life ever), I applied for a few sought after organisations for campus placements. The initial tests were simple enough and I made into a shortlist for two companies and was eagerly awaiting the interview process while nurturing my dream to be an entrepreneur eventually.

I land my first big interview with a leading insurance company, and I begin to research the job profile and learn almost everything about the company through publicly available information (internet was not an integral part of our lives back then). I borrowed a blue suit from a friend and was dressed to impress in a white shirt underneath (till today I hate to wear a tie but guess that's irrelevant to the story or may be not).

On the day of the interview 22nd July 2001, I drove to Connaught place – (Central Business District of New

Delhi) to make sure I have enough time to navigate the busy roads of Delhi where road rules seldom apply.

After a thirty-minute struggle to find a parking spot on a dusty road, I make my way to the building and was mesmerised by the architecture and design of the building and my mind starts to envision my life as a hot shot corporate honcho in a couple of years with my interview with a picture in leading business magazines.

I take a busy lift and promptly announce myself to the concierge table with a view of the city, my first thought is how on earth did my city look so breathtaking from a fifty fourth floor? Is this the same city which is always dusty and full of people with crowded roads with barely a place to breathe at ease? My chain of thought is interrupted by a Human Resource representative named Niti who introduces herself and the interview process and leads me to a conference room which already seated about twenty other applicants.

I am called in at 11:03 am and panel of four senior members of the team greeted me with firm handshakes, having taken a seat and handed them a copy of my curriculum vitae (and yes, those were the time of hard copy CV's) from my leather folder. After answering a series of general questions regarding my interests, reason for applying for a role of an underwriter and my family composition, I mentally prepare myself to receive an appointment letter right there.

Truth be told, I did not know what an underwriter did till a week ago, thanks to my friend's brother who used to work in the field, I learned enough to explain the role at a high level.

When enquired about my future plans, I casually mention that after a couple of years I plan to may be pursue an MBA. I assumed this will impress the interview panel, but I cannot explain how ludicrous that assumption turns out to be, the senior most gentleman told me with a poker face "you are a chicken and not the pig" and we are looking for pigs to join our prestigious organisation. Looking at my bewildered expression, he softened a bit and explained the story which goes as follows:

One day the chicken decides that the two should start a restaurant.

The pig is intrigued by the idea and says, "That sounds great. I'm an entrepreneurial type of hog. I'm sick of working for the farmer. But what are we going to call the restaurant?"

The chicken thinks. Then she scratches and pecks at the dirt and suggests, "Ham and Eggs!"

To which the pig replies, "No thanks, I'd be committed. You'd only be involved."

I take a pause and try to soak the story in and decide something impressive to say but my mind raced in different directions and said, "though I love bacon, but I prefer chicken due the variety it has to offer". Still not fully comprehending that the story draws insight towards commitment and involvement which I will learn a little later in life. Couple of other formal questions later, the interview ended and as expected I never received a call further.

I narrate this incident to couple of my close friends and though none of them could extract the hidden wisdom out of it, they were all sure that we need to be prepared for unexpected questions like these during the interview process.

Feeling a little demotivated and lost in life again, I went out for dinner with my family and tell them that the interview went well since my parents, either brother or sister had no experience in facing interviews or corporate lives. I came from a family of entrepreneurs who felt working for others is nothing short of a mediocre way of earning a livelihood.

May be everyone in my family was a pig and I was heading in a way of becoming a chicken? I decide to leave this analogy and focus on pizzas and garlic breads on the table before my siblings grab the best pieces. On the way back home, my dad casually asks me again to join the growing family's grocery business which had significant expansion opportunities. Not wanting to get into debate again, I say, let me think about it but thanks for the offer.

Next Wednesday my interview is scheduled with a relatively well-known bank in Gurgaon (a satellite city adjacent to New Delhi and home to significant international organisations), I spend my entire weekend preparing for the interview. I had applied for a role of a management trainee, not 100% sure of what that entailed, I ask around anyone and everyone and got varied answers. I decide to go with an open mind and be myself instead of rehearsing impressive answers and try too hard to get the job instead.

My drive to Gurgaon from New Delhi was excruciating with endless traffic, bumpy roads and impatient drivers and took over ninety minutes with a constant struggle to save my humble car from drivers who believe following roads rules are optional.

Gurgaon resembles like a global city like New York or Hong Kong from what I saw in movies since I have never flown overseas, I was remarkably impressed and prayed for this job as I entered a seventy-floor glass tower in the shape of a ship.

Promptly at 1:20 pm, I announced myself to the concierge for my 1:30 PM interview meeting – YES I am always punctual and I hate last minute scrambling. The interview process was behind schedule and after waiting for forty minutes, my name is called upon and an impressive human resource manager named Lisa who shakes my hand and introduces herself while leading me to the glass conference room at the same time.

Believe me at that time I am more interested to get to know Lisa than getting a job. I quickly gain my composure and take a seat, after initial pleasantries were exchanged. Interview begins courteously and I am asked a series of questions like:

What skills do I bring to this role?

Where do I see yourself in 5 years?

Why do I want to join banking?

I answer these questions being myself and then the last question stunned me.

"Would you prefer to be a specialist in one area of the business and increase depth of your experience or gain exposure across different areas and focus on breadth of experience instead"?

I take a pause and my mind race towards the previous interview question on being a Pig versus Chicken and get uncomfortable. I hear an inner voice that says based on my previous experience, they would prefer me to be a pig and hence I should say depth of experience so that I can be committed to the job. I still don't know why but I decide to be myself instead and answer with confidence.

"I would prefer to learn my current role deeply and then to move on to a new role to broaden my experience and skill set".

Though I am unable to read the interview's expression, I am satisfied with my answer and prepared for the result to go either way. They do not ask any further questions and give me an overview of the bank, the working culture and high-level expectations of the role.

Next morning, as I am getting ready to meet my friend and watch a movie, I receive a call from the bank's human resource department and get invited back to the company at 2:30 pm. I am excited about the prospect of getting a job and properly start my corporate career, I cancel my program and get dress formally and start driving to Gurgaon at around 1 pm to ensure adequate time to account for crazy drivers and packed roads.

I announce myself at the concierge promptly at 2:15 pm and took a seat, at sharp 2:30 pm, the same gorgeous human resource manager "Lisa" walked in and shakes my hand and congratulate me on getting the job. I almost begin to hug her in excitement, but someone restrain myself and thank her.

We both walk into a spotless glass conference room with a massive table which can accommodate a town where she offers me some water and begins giving me an overview of the job expectations and entitlements of the role. This was followed by the most anticipated moment of my corporate career when she hands me the fourteen page "offer letter" printed on a crisp letter head and smelled like a treasure. She requests me to read the terms of the employment and sign a copy for company records and acknowledgment and walks out of the room to provide me the privacy.

My excitement gets the better of me and I cannot concentrate on the details of employment terms, I just glance on page 11 which details my compensation and potential yearly bonus and incentive details and was happy with what was printed. I sign the document within three minutes and envision myself as senior executive of this bank with an enclosed office making more money than I can ever spend and a beautiful secretary, a company provided house, car and a driver.

A fortnight later, my official corporate journey begins with incredible learning opportunities almost daily. One of the core questions still lingers my mind:

"Should one be a Pig or a Chicken"?

Chapter 7

Happiness Quotient

It's a beautiful summer Friday in Sydney, Australia late afternoon and a group of nine bookworms meet in a quite part of an otherwise crowded bar overlooking the stunning Opera House on the right and mesmerizing Sydney Harbour Bridge on my left. As I notice the flurry of passengers with colourful luggages disembarking a massive Ovation by the Sea cruise, it's hard not to notice the excitement on people's faces. My jealous streak is broken by a pint of pacific ale beer on tap screaming to be sipped, there are few things better than a first sip of fresh beer believe me – I say it from experience.

I have been an avid reader for years and an active part of a book club that meets once month to discuss and deliberate about a pre-selected book followed by drinks and delicious food continuing the uninhabited discussion about varied topics without judgement.

Melissa, the book club leader starts the format of the club with customary introductions for new members and introduces a thought instead of a book this time to share our thoughts on.

"Wanting to be happy leads to unhappiness".

This thought ties a knot in my brain, and I can see similar expression on other faces. This is the longest pause in the history of this book club, I try and break the silence by saying "isn't wanting to be happy essential to be happy", in other words how can I be happy without wanting to be happy? Another long silence thereby pushing the group to focus on alcohol instead of the topic at hand.

I get an impression that after working for more than 60 hours a week, most of us are not prepared for this heavy topic. The meeting concludes without much of discussion which is unusual in a group where its not uncommon to wait a considerable time to get a chance to share your thoughts and opinion.

As I enter the busy Wynyard station to board my train back home, my mind is still preoccupied with thoughts, and I keep imagining whether each person I cross on the subway is happy or not. The moment reminds me of certain key moments of my life when I felt truly happy, but was that true happiness or was it just a mirage? As I board my train on platform 4 and settle on a window seat, I feel an unusual calm, as if my mind is thoughtless which is not a feeling I am used to generally.

My life has been full of milestones and targets which led me to believe that achieving these milestones is a definition of happiness. Some of these targets included:

1. Owning my first bike

2. Getting my first job

3. Earning a specified sum of money

4. Travelling

5. Learning a new skill

6. Finding my life partner

7. Owning my first home

Though all these milestones when achieved contributed a great deal of value in my life, over the period of time I realised that this is not a barometer of true happiness. These achievements though are important to grow and learn but are not in direct alignment of true happiness.

The more I read about topic like happiness depends on Self, problems with concepts like pursuit of happiness and specially with scientific research proving the role of limbic system of the brain etc. Somehow scientific analysis on a topic like "what makes and or keeps me happy seemed complicated and farfetched and often contradictory to each other". This made me believe that being happy is complex and difficult for me to understand and appreciate.

I am preparing myself to disembark at my station to realise its raining and I am not carrying my umbrella, normally a situation like this would bother me and I would curse or blame myself for not being prepared. However, with so much going on in my mind, I keep walking towards my home completely oblivious to the pour.

Happiness, like other emotions, is not something we achieve, but rather something we inhabit. It is temporary. Always.

What this means is that finding happiness is not achieved in itself, but rather it is the side effect of a particular set of ongoing life experiences. This gets mixed up a lot, especially since happiness is marketed so much these days as a goal in and of itself. Buy X and be happy. Learn Y and be happy. But you can't buy happiness and you can't achieve happiness. It just is—once you get other parts of your life in order.

I think, when we seek happiness, we are actually seeking pleasure: good food, more sex, more time for TV and movies, a new car, parties with friends, more likes on social media, full body massages, losing 10 pounds, becoming more popular, and so on.

But while pleasure is great, it's not the same as happiness. Pleasure can be correlated with happiness but does not cause it.

Happiness is a moment before you need more happiness:

Over the years of achieving milestones in my personal and professional life, I realised that happiness is precisely the moment before you realise you need something else to be happy now.

Over the years I have experienced an inherent paradox of expectations which are often key to happiness in the modern world".

"If I only wish to be happy, it can be easily accomplished, but if I want to be happier than others who seem happier than they are, it's IMPOSSIBLE".

Chapter 8

Focus on what Never Changes

One thing common about almost every meeting, get together, media debates, articles etc is focus on what is ever changing......new ways of working, new technologies, diets, workout regimens, fashion trends, payments and the list is endless. I have spent hundreds of hours researching new trends to potentially invest in companies in the field, learn new technologies at work and generally to keep abreast of latest in the world.

One thing common about these advancements is that they become a new normal and it is relatively difficult to go back to the time they did not exist. Great examples of these include streaming TV and smart phones. Though I vividly remember the days of appointment television with irritating ad breaks, I cannot envisage going back to that era. Same is the case with wall phones and pre smart phones.

Whilst the world is changing constantly and we do not know who is inventing a new potential way of disruption in their tiny garage right now, it's imperative to understand few things that never change. I realised this when I came across an interview of Jeff Bezos – founder of Amazon which revolutionized the way we shop.

He says "I very frequently get the question: 'What's going to change in the next 10 years?' And that is a very interesting question; it's a very common one. I almost never get the question:

'What's not going to change in the next 10 years?' And I submit to you that that second question is actually the more important of the two -- because you can build a business strategy around the things that are stable in time. ... In our retail business, we know that customers want low prices, and I know that's going to be true 10 years from now.

They want fast delivery; they want vast selection. It's impossible to imagine a future 10 years from now where a customer comes up and says, 'Jeff I love Amazon; I just wish the prices were a little higher,' [or] 'I love Amazon; I just wish you'd deliver a little more slowly.' Impossible. And so the effort we put into those things, spinning those things up, we know the energy we put into it today will still be paying off dividends for our customers 10 years from now.

When you have something that you know is true, even over the long term, you can afford to put a lot of energy into it."

– Jeff Bezos

Another great insight from the world's most famous investor:

In 2009, during the peak of The Great Recession, Warren Buffett was driving through downtown Omaha, Neb., with a CEO friend, who took note of their bleak surroundings: Empty streets, shuttered shops, a future with seemingly little hope.

"Warren, how are we ever going to pull out of this?", the friend asked. "This country is never going to be the same."

Buffett paused, then posed a question.

"Do you know what the best-selling candy bar was in 1962?"

When the friend said he wasn't sure, Buffett told him it was Snickers. Then, he told him what the best-selling candy bar was now: Snickers.

This has a deep wisdom specially when everything seems to change with an advent of artificial intelligence, fear of robots taking over jobs. However, it contains a valuable lesson for all of us as well and reminds us that some fundamentals never change.

With the end of 2024 drawing closer, some of us are likely frustrated by undesired change, lamenting our bad luck, growing a bit cynical of the circumstances surrounding our teams and our work.

It is natural to feel frustrated by quantum of change around us with futurists painting a potentially bleak future of humanity where working with be optional and every human being paid a universal basic income.

But what we likely aren't giving as much weight to that perhaps we should are the constants of our lives and our teams, the factors that will go untouched, what can withstand turbulence and upheaval.

There may be some new faces, there may be new technology in place or team members who need serious moulding.

But the job, the goals and the methods to achieve these will largely remain the same time and time again, despite the inevitable peaks and valleys of our work lives.

Buffett's point with the Snickers wasn't to ignore reality or to be a delusional optimist about the bleak circumstances surrounding the country at the time.

It was that amidst the hardship and the obstacles, there are also plenty of elements that don't waiver.

And it's these constants that almost always allow us to prevail.

Let's focus our attention to markets, my close friend Alex Steward is a career investor who has stood the test of time when it comes to getting consistent returns for his clients. His fund has never been rated amongst the best performing or top 10 funds. However, he has a track record of providing average returns of north of sixteen percentage consistently for the last 14 years.

His approach to building his and his client's wealth can be summarized as follows:

1. No one can predict the bull and bear runs hence there is no perfect time to start investing.

2. The best financial plan is to save like a pessimist and invest like an optimist.

3. Power of compounding – Even ordinary returns compounded for a long period of time create extraordinary returns.

Despite the constant changes in technology, fashion, markets and trends, some things will never change, and these are the fundamentals to double down on.

Chapter 9

Power of Storytelling

*If you have the right answer, you may or may
not get ahead. If you have the wrong answer
but you're a good storyteller, you'll probably get ahead
(for a while). If you have the right answer and
you're a good storyteller, you'll almost
certainly get ahead…*
Morgan Housel in Same as Ever

In my professional and personal life, I have always preferred to take a fact or data-based approach. My thinking is guided by the saying "data or facts never lie" or "facts or data are indisputable". In my professional life, I have had a great deal of success with this approach as majority of my business cases or project ideas have been endorsed. However, not all projects saw the light of the day and went into a pile of prioritisation without funding being approved to start immediately.

My colleague and mentor named Smithesh Manoharan had a different way of presentation which was stitching a dream or helping senior stakeholders imagine what future can potentially look like. He would resist sharing numbers, facts, data and financial impacts wherever possible but more often than not, come out of the meeting with an endorsement backed with funding.

I had a frank conversation with him one day when we were traveling together on work.

We both are at an overseas conference in Orlando USA and after a series of boring presentations, lectures, and discussions later, we decide to go out for drinks at the hotel bar called Morocco.

The bar is packed, dark and loud so we decide to take a quite table outside and ordered two Old Fashioned cocktails. After years of feeling a sense of admiration and jealousy towards him, I decide to seek his help and learn an effective way to create a solid narrative and secure project funding. I say out loud, Smithesh I have worked with you side by side and at times worked extra hard to build business cases with irrefutable facts, data, financial numbers including cost benefit analysis and everything in between but you have a much better success rate of getting your projects initiated, does it seem fair to you? Be honest.

As our drinks arrive, his gaze shifts to a cute waitress who brings our drinks. After few moments of silence, we toast to a great career we both have built over a period. After a quick first sip of his Old Fashion, he says "Ankush, you are one of the most diligent professional and you always make sure you have an accurate answer to almost any question with data during a meeting". However, you tend to miss narrating a story. I say with a confused expression, I am neither a writer nor in an entertainment business to tell great stories.

Almost expecting my answer, he takes another sip and says, "facts are forgotten, stories are memorable". This reminds me of a famous quote I read recently in a book I cannot remember now:

"Value of a company = numbers of today multiplied by story of tomorrow"

It's not what you say, it's how?

Corporate lesson:

Once upon a time, Jack and Max are walking to the church for the Sunday prayer.

Jack wonders whether it would be all right to smoke while praying.

Max replies, "Why don't you ask the Priest?"

So Jack goes up to the Priest and asks, "Father, may I smoke while I pray?"

The Priest replies, "No, my son, you may not! That's utter disrespect to our religion."

Jack goes back to his friend and tells him what the good Priest told him.

Max says, "I'm not surprised. You asked the wrong question. Let me try."

And so Max goes up to the Priest and asks, "Father, may I pray while I smoke?"

To which the Priest eagerly replies, "By all means, my son. By all means. You can always pray whenever you want to."

Moral of the story

The approval you want depends on the way u ask for it!!

Chapter 10

Choosing When to Choose

Every alternate weekend, me and my best friend & wife spend a better part our Sunday volunteering at a local church in Sydney, Australia. As a part of fundraising program, we partner with local producers and sell their produce post the Sunday sermons around noon. The church thoughtfully and graciously arranges a crèche for babies and kids to support parents devote their attention to weekly bible lessons and we regularly drop our toddler son to play and learn there which adds to the incentive of fundraising.

It is a chilly and unusually wet weekend of July as we struggle to find a parking spot at a busy neighbourhood community centre, the community centre is unusually busy with multiple local activities and sessions concurrently. After dropping our son to the play area, we meet with a local farmer and collect the cartons full of locally produced honey at a beautiful neighbourhood farm located in Glenorie.

Since it is a busy weekend, me and my wife decide to host the honey counters at the opposite end of the community centre to attract maximum number of patrons. I had instructed the farmer to drop as many varieties of honey as possible for tasting at the event. As we set our respective tables at the opposite ends, I meticulously showcase sixteen different varieties to include manuka, orange peel, hazelnut blend, berry blossom to name a few with disposable spoons to encourage patrons to taste as many as possible before buying. My wife decides to offer only four varieties of honey for tasting and I tell myself, I will raise at least double the funds for the church compared to the opposite end.

It is a little past noon, and patrons start passing by the stalls and I great them enthusiastically and offer a trial. At the end of the event, before collecting our son who was busy assembling a wiggles puzzle, we reconciled our experiences.

To my utter surprise, at my table each patron approximately tasted six varieties of honey on an average and about twenty percent of those actually made a purchase. At an opposite end, at my wife's table, average tasting was two per person and more than forty five percent ended up making a purchase. Though, we both raise upwards of four thousand dollars for a great cause and are delighted of our effort and contribution, I cannot not decipher the results.

Doesn't more choice encourage a customer to buy more?

Why do organisations across almost every industry and product type offer a vast number of varieties?

Coincidently, we do our grocery and fresh produce shopping for a week on a Sunday as well which is my responsibility and I fulfill that with pride. We grab lunch at a local café, and I drop my wife and my monster home and decide to complete weekly ritual of grocery shopping.

At my local shopping mart, I am usually an expert in deciding instantly which aisles to skip and which ones to never miss for a chance to try newly introduced products. Strangely, today's shopping experience seems different (may be my earlier experience of a choice dilemma had something to do with it).

I try to ignore my mind's chatter and head to an aisle 8 to get fresh eggs, normally I blindly pick up two cartons of extra-large cage free farm eggs. Today for some reason, I notice there are approximately twenty-three different varieties of eggs to choose from ranging from but not limited to cage eggs, cage free, large, extra-large, double yolk, barn raised, farm raised to name a few. Within an umbrella of cage free eggs, choice is available to choose from the farm or a barn density for example not more than one thousand chickens per a hectare of farm and beyond.

To make it further complex, all the above varieties are equally available with the supermarket own brand umbrella and with multiple external brands some of which are household names.

I end up buying the same eggs I have been buying from the same supermarket for more than eight years, but the choice seemed difficult today.

Next, I move my trolley to isle four to buy some biscuits and cookies for my son, for the first time, I made a mental note on varieties of biscuits spread out on four long Aisles. There are approximately forty-one kinds of salted crackers for me to choose from. I am mentally fatigued with these options and just picked up the one he likes.

Speaking of supermarkets, I cannot help but give you another marketing masterpiece to sell more of the same product. One of the world's largest dairy companies introduced a healthy version of yoghurt with just five percent of fat compared to a regular yoghurt and spent considerable marketing dollars to promote it through social media with local and international influencers promoting the product extensively to their followers.

To their disbelief, the seemingly healthy yoghurt did not sell much in spite of their research proving that there is a significant need of this segment referred as healthy yoghurt. The company changed their strategy to rebrand the same yoghurt variant by striking off "five percent fat" and changing the label to mention "ninety five percent fat free". They saw a jump in sales by 34 percent within a month and remained stable from thereon. The product remained exactly same with five percent fat compared to regular yoghurt which essentially meant its ninety five percent fat free.

THE PARADOX OF CHOICE

TOO MUCH CHOICE LEADS TO PARALYSIS AND DISSATISFACTION

Now let us talk about how companies use innovative marketing techniques to lure us into making a decision beneficial to them by making it feel like you as a customer have got the best deal. Let me illustrate a personal example from the electronics industry, moving away from supermarkets for a moment.

We have been wanting to buy a new robot vacuum cleaner for a while since our professional commitments and caring for our little one leaves almost no time for these household chores. My wife researched for the best make and models and we made a trip our nearby mall to scout for best deals. The model we shortlisted was quoted anywhere between $1,975 to $2,230 by different stores post negotiation. We mutually decided that it's an expensive purchase on top of our fortnightly professional cleaning arrangements already in place and decide not to buy it.

A fortnight later, my wife and son attended a kid's birthday party in the same mall. After dropping our son to enjoy the birthday rides with his friends, my wife decides to visit that appliance store again just to browse and essentially kill sometime while waiting for the party to finish. She notices a further latest model of the same brand with eight additional minutes of battery life and a newly introduced colour (blue) not available before and was priced at $3,199.

Suddenly our previously shortlisted model seemed reasonably priced to her and she immediately called me from the store and said "I have decided to buy the robot vacuum we shortlisted for $1,975 since its economically priced against the new model and as per her it was a deal too good to be missed. To be honest, we do not regret making that purchase since its really handy and saves us valuable time, it's a fact that an expensive purchase can seem a great value if an anchoring point (reference rate) shifts. Perfect example of anchoring.

Let me illustrate another example to ascertain an impact of reference rate our choice. I was in Hong-

Kong for a conference last month with my colleague and we decided to explore local cuisine extensively. Every evening, we would venture out on the streets of central Hong-Kong to try local delicacies, and "Sai Kung Seafood Street" caught my attention. While ordering a shrimp papaya noodle salad, there was a small A5 size black & white poster mentioning:

Shrimp Papaya Noodle salad $19.50 (cash) and $19.90 (by card)

We both ordered our respective salads and grabbed a plastic table with two not so clean chairs to relish our food with a Hong-Kong style milk tea which is a signature beverage of the place. We both had different interpretation of the same dish priced differently depending on how you pay. My colleague assumed he got a discount of $0.40 by paying through cash as his reference price was $19.90. Since I did not have local currency notes, I assumed I have paid a surcharge of $0.40 for paying through my credit card.

Depending on your reference price, you can either be pleased with an assumed discount or unhappy for being asked to pay a surcharge.

Chapter 11

The World Today is a much better place than what media wants you to believe...

*News is about things that happen,
not things that don't happen. We never see a
journalist saying to the camera, "I'm reporting
live from a country where war has not broken out" –
or a city that has not been bombed, or a school
that has not been shot up......*
Steven Pinker

We are no strangers to constant rhetoric that the world as we know is deteriorating due to ever increasing population resulting in global warming and other natural calamities like earthquakes and floods. The phrase global warming was one of most searched phrases in the online searches for years, though there are some trends to indicate its impact, what gets completely missed are the positive changes the world has witnessed.

It is a well-known and researched fact that bad news spreads and sells more or should we say is shared and commented more in the age of social media resulting in more eyeballs leading to increase in ad revenues due to black box algorithms.

Let's discuss some of the world's significant challenges and try to analyse them with right perspective which makes all the difference.

1. Child Mortality rate

What if I were to tell you that despite massive improvements in medical science and general living conditions across the world, by 2010, only 80% of the children survived to the age of 5. This is a tragedy by any standards if we rely solely on this data point.

Now let's shift the perspective by comparing the 80% survival rate in 2010 to just 58% in the year 1975. Now that a significant improvement of 22% in 35 years. Does this change your perspective slightly about this subject?

Hindsight's big lesson is that things change – in this case improve. But it is hard to imagine how dire living conditions were in the past.

CHILD CANCER SURVIVAL

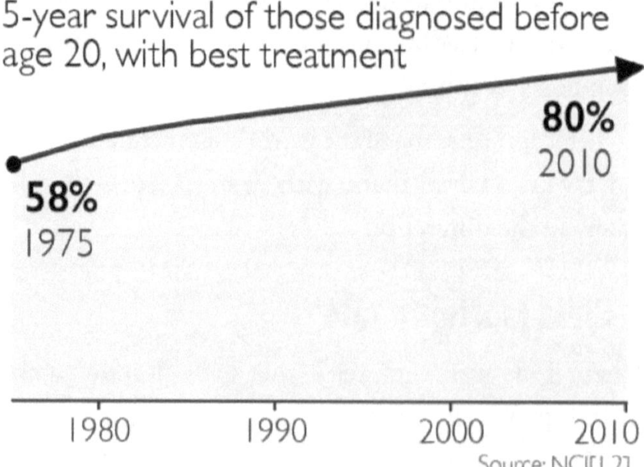

Now let's look at the latest available data up to 2020, does it change your perspective completely?

The world is much better

Data: 2020 data from UN IGME and historical data from Volk and Atkinson (2013).

2. Pollution

Despite improvements in manufacturing processes, improved emission norms & appliances and power generation through wind and solar sources, the problem of pollution seems to be worse than ever before. Whilst the effects of pollution are being felt more acutely than ever before, this rhetoric misses an important indicator that suggests reduction of smoke particles per person by 2/3rd when compared from 1970 to 2010.

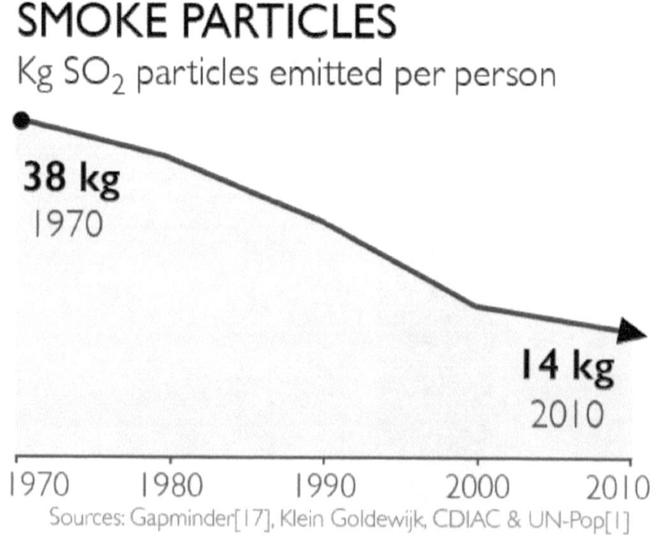

3. Population

Growing population across the world and its potential repercussions is a regular worry, more so since the assumption is that the population will continue to grow at the same pace. This presumption is not true, because as per UN forecasts, the world population will peak lower (at 8.9 billion) and sooner (by 2060) than earlier forecasts and will decline to 7.8 billion people by the end of the century. The significant decline in fertility rates in most nations means that global population will not continue forever on a runaway upward trajectory but will ultimately drop below its current level.

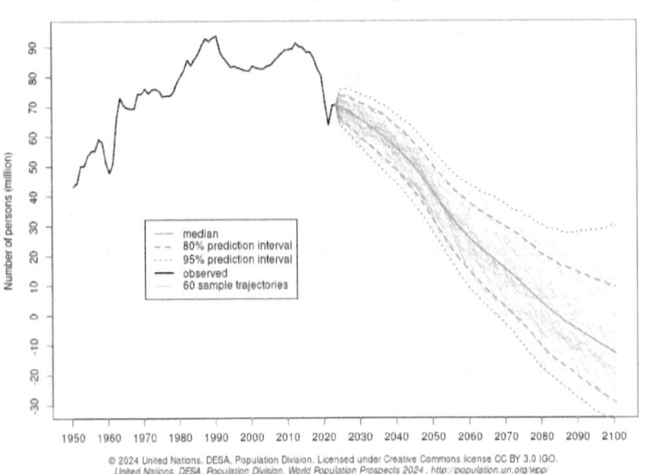

4. Resources

Coal, crude oil and even water availability is expected to become dire as per certain section of intellectuals across the world. Despite these claims, humanity has not run out of a single supposedly non-renewable resource. Fossil fuels and most minerals are more abundant than in the past. Indeed, most resources are so plentiful they will last for centuries. There are compelling reasons to challenge the claims of resource depletion. To add to this, we can already see innovations like electric vehicles and gradual but substantial shifts to renewal energy across the world is leading to significant reduction in the demand of fossil fuels and minerals.

5. The world economy

The size of the world's economy has grown more than a hundredfold over the past two centuries. Economic growth leads to higher average incomes, enabling consumers to buy more goods and services and enjoy better standards of living. If global economic growth maintains its 2.8 per cent average rate since 2000, GDP will increase to a whopping $1.1 quadrillion by 2100.

6. End of Famine

Famines have all but disappeared outside of war zones. Adequate nutrition is a basic requirement for human survival, yet throughout history, food has always been scarce. Today, the world's poorest region (Sub-Saharan Africa) enjoys access to food that is equivalent to that of the Portuguese in the early 1960s.

7. More land for nature

The global tree canopy increased by 2.24 million square kilometres between 1982 and 2016. This equates to seven-per-cent of the Earth's surface covered by new trees. Mother nature is beating deforestation resulting in expanding woodlands. There are just over three trillion trees on our planet – that's roughly 422 trees for every person on Earth.

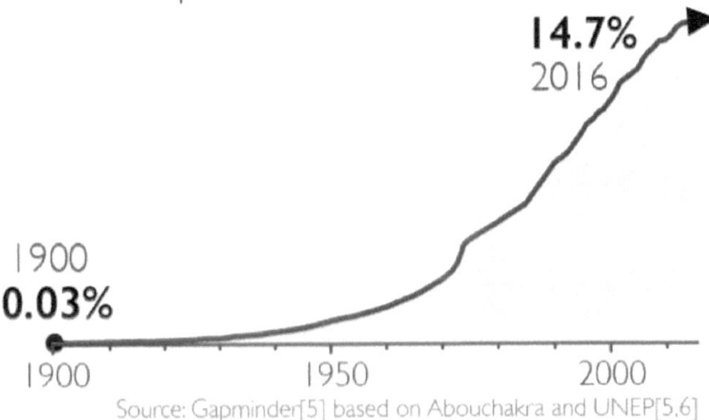

8. A Safer World

The chances of a person dying in a natural catastrophe – earthquake, flood, drought, epidemic, etc. – has declined by nearly 99 per cent over the past century. Today, buildings are better constructed to survive earthquakes, weather satellites provide early storm warnings, and swift medical interventions limit the spread of diseases.

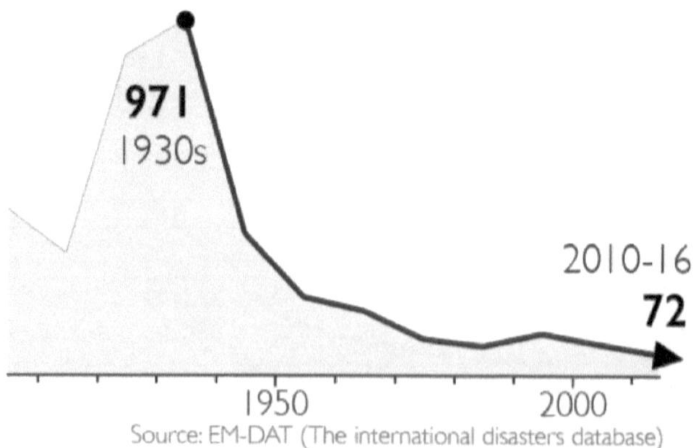

The world in general is by far better then before across all key areas, but that fact rarely gets mentioned by the media since it does not attract many eye balls and hence advertising dollars.

Clearly, the world is not going to the dogs and these are not bleak times. Almost everywhere you turn, you can find evidence of some positive trend – if you are prepared to look. The remaining 68 trends outlined in Ten Global Trends show that on all key dimensions of human well-being, the world is in an extraordinarily better place today than just a few decades ago.

Most people are better educated, better fed, more literate, and have more life options than at any other time in human history. Incomes and life expectancy are rising while child mortality and cancer death rates are falling.

Stocks of nuclear warheads have plummeted and digital technology has transformed how we live, work, and play.

The world isn't as horrific as we have been led to believe. Indeed, there's never been a better time to be alive. In bygone years, life was shorter, sicker, poorer, more dangerous, and less free. So, we need to stop bingeing on bad news and seek out the positives in the world as good news lifts our spirits. We should also follow the advice of the Monty Python song – Always Look on the Bright Side of Life.

And if you want to appreciate the simple things in daily life, just listen to the lyrics of Louis Armstrong's song – What a Wonderful World.

Chapter 12

Experience Economy

We are all in search of great experiences – be it in watching movies with ultra-high definition and Dolby Atmos surround sound or buying a latest car with almost full self-driving capabilities or the latest model of mobile phone which can almost read your mind.

The experience economy phase was invented and made famous by Joseph Pine when he released his book by the same name in year 2011. I have had a great privilege of attending one of his presentations and talks in Orlando United Stated in year 2020 which was a trigger for me to research more about experience economy in general.

In his book "the Experience Economy", Joseph Pine categorises an offering in to four distinct categories:

1. Commodity

2. Good

3. Service &

4. Experience

Consider a true commodity: the coffee bean. Companies that harvest coffee or trade it on the futures market receive – at the time of this writing – a little more than seventy-five cents per pound, which translates into one or two cents a cup. When a manufacturer roasts, grinds, packages, and sells those same beans in a grocery store, turning them into a good, the price to a consumer jump between five and twenty-five cents a cup (depending on brand and package size). Brew the ground beans in a run-of-the-mill diner, quick-serve restaurant or bodega, and that coffee making service now sells for fifty cents to a dollar per cup.

So depending on what a business does with it, coffee can be any of the three economic offerings – commodity, good, or service – with three distinct ranges of value customers attach to the offering. But wait: serve that same coffee in a five-star restaurant or a café such as Starbucks- where the ordering, creation and consumption of the cup embody a heightened ambience or sense of theatre- and consumers gladly pay $2 to $5 a cup. Businesses that ascend to this fourth level of value establish a distinctive experience that envelops the purchase of coffee, increasing its value (and therefore its price) by two orders of magnitude over the original commodity.

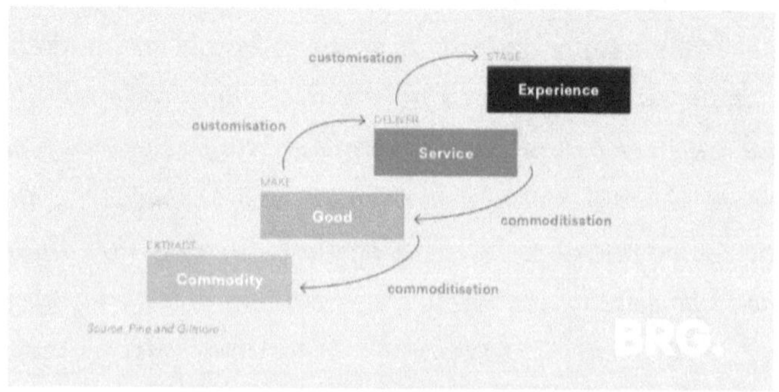

Another example of experience economy curated by restaurants takes it to a completely different level, let me illustrate it with a real-life example.

Hawaii, Honolulu is one of my favourite destinations in the world and me and my wife travelled there for two weeks a couple years ago. Oahu island is home to some great food and other experience, and we also happened to meet our old friends outside the Cheesecake Factory. They were coincidently holidaying there at the same time with their kids, and we decided to have a lazy dinner together the next day. They were planning a Mexican dinner and suggested one of the most recommended restaurants not too far from our hotel and me and my wife happily agreed on the cuisine since we both cherish a good Mexican meal.

Next evening, we promptly meet at seven thirty outside the Mexican restaurant whose tagline was "make eating out into an experience worth remembering" with a picture of a happy couple overjoyed experiencing a chef preparing a dish on their table. As we greet our friends, I casually mention that I am looking forward to an amazing culinary experience today just like a couple in this picture and smiled.

The restaurant was impeccably designed with minimalist and yet practical décor and mood lighting, and a live band dressed in Hawaiian attire instilling local touch and were dressed to impressed. We order our respective dishes and drinks, and the waiter recommends that we try one of the most ordered dishes in the menu titled "live guacamole" and the menu reads as follows:

Guacamole *(mashed, raw avocados mixed with other ingredients to taste)-* $6.00

Live Guacamole *(all the above, prepared just for you in front of your eyes)* $15.00

Our curiosity peaks and we decide to order "live guacamole" expecting to feel ecstatic as the couple on the picture outside the restaurant must have felt.

Our drinks arrive and we toast to our holiday and bumping to each other at this breathtaking city reminiscing our travel experiences so far and a chef dressed in a traditional chef uniform arrives on our table. The chef begins to prepare the "live guacamole" by peeling a perfectly ripe avocado and mashes the same with a traditional wooden spoon, adds fresh lemon juice, Spanish onion, coriander and few homemade spices. Our chef neatly serves the dish in a silver bowl and says "bon appetite" and proceeds to walk towards the kitchen may be to recreate the experience for another table in need of a same overpaid and overhyped experience.

Once we finish the dinner and truth be told the food was undoubtfully delicious, I could not help thinking about how unrequired the experience of live guacamole actually turned out to be. The conversation for that five-minutes had to be compromised with absolutely no improvement in the taste of a kitchen prepared guacamole.

This leads me to conclude these notable things:

1. Not every presumed different experience will be valuable.

2. People will value each experience differently basis the perceived value it adds to their time at that precise moment.

3. Taste and quality are the greatest barometer for a restaurant compared to whether a dish is prepared in the kitchen or within two feet of your eyes.

4. Choose experiences that are valuable to yourself vs what the influencers are selling you on social media.

Chapter 13

The efficiency trap / Slow down to speed up

The significant part of my professional life (upwards of fifteen years) has been spent or utilized in generating or implementing ideas to add efficiency to corporates covering systems, processes, people, automation opportunities and the list is endless. My professional experiences led me to plan and execute almost every activity including mundane day to day tasks like unloading a dishwasher into an opportunity to save few minutes. My brain analyses not only the shortest route to drive to my gym (depending on the time of the day of course) but also which road lanes to avoid minimizing the need to slow down while giving way to merging traffic.

I have also analysed the best time of the day to workout saving me fifteen minutes on an average per day which I would potentially waste due to lift delays and waiting for workout machines to be free. When working out of office, I either have an early or late lunch helping me avoid overcrowding in the lifts and my local food court and I almost always pre order through an app ahead of time.

My obsession to efficiency reached its crescendo when I felt guilty of sitting idle on the park bench while my son was enjoying his rides in our local park. I almost always carry a book during these times, which I forgot on that particular day. Though I relish every minute spent with my family, the task of waiting for my son to finish the ride seemed inefficient to me.

Efficiency can also hamper creativity, a very different but pertinent view from Jerry Seinfeld (one of the best comedians of our time) during an interview with Harvard Business Review.

HBR: You and Larry David wrote Seinfeld together, without a traditional writers' room, and burnout was one reason you stopped. Was there a more sustainable way to do it? Could McKinsey or someone have helped you find a better model?

Seinfeld: Who's McKinsey?

HBR: It's a consulting firm.

Seinfeld: Are they funny?

HBR: No.

Seinfeld: Then I don't need them. If you're efficient, you're doing it the wrong way. The right way is the hard way. The show was successful because I micromanaged it—every word, every line, every take, every edit, every casting. That's my way of life.

My Favorite line:

"The right way is the hard way".

Chapter 14

Postponing what truly matters in your life.........

I started working fairly early in my life and for reasons unknown to me, my priority was always to work doubly hard, grow in my professional life, make tonnes of money and then retire by the time I reach an age of forty-five. This was my mantra and I almost dreamed about it daily and that kept me going for more than fifteen long years in the corporate life. I always wanted to travel the world and experience what life has to offer across the globe and had a long bucket list of places to visit but my constant need to make more money and work ridiculous hours daily to be ahead of others and reach a magical saving and investment number before I turn forty-five.

I was almost on track of my financial goals with my investments in real estate, equity through electronic traded funds and direct portfolio in shares ensuring diversification. Back of my mind from the age of thirty-five, discontentment steadily crept making me feel a tinge of FOMO (fear of missing out). While my colleagues and friends were constantly sharing the stories of their escapades of an Italian summer to a wild African safari and all I could discuss is the next big idea to grow my portfolio.

The strange part of my dream was that I always dreamed of a quiet and peaceful life post my hypothetical retirement contrary to other people I knew. My future imagination had the following:

1. Health and family

2. A tiny house on the beach in a small town

3. Tonnes of books

4. A small car

5. Pantry full of healthy food

Until a friend of mine forwarded me this story:

There was once a businessman who was sitting by the beach in a small Brazilian village.

As he sat, he saw a Brazilian fisherman rowing a small boat towards the shore having caught quite few big fish.

The businessman was impressed and asked the fisherman, "How long does it take you to catch so many fish?"

The fisherman replied, "Oh, just a short while."

"Then why don't you stay longer at sea and catch even more?" The businessman was astonished.

"This is enough to feed my whole family," the fisherman said.

The businessman then asked, "So, what do you do for the rest of the day?"

The fisherman replied, "Well, I usually wake up early in the morning, go out to sea and catch a few fish, then go back and play with my kids. In the afternoon, I take a nap with my wife, and evening comes, I join my buddies in the village for a drink — we play guitar, sing and dance throughout the night."

The businessman offered a suggestion to the fisherman.

"I am a PhD in business management. I could help you to become a more successful person. From now on, you should spend more time at sea and try to catch as many fish as possible. When you have saved enough money, you could buy a bigger boat and catch even more fish. Soon you will be able to afford to buy more boats, set up your own company, your own production plant for canned food and distribution network. By then, you will have moved out of this village and to Sao Paulo, where you can set up HQ to manage your other branches."

The fisherman continues, "And after that?"

The businessman laughs heartily, "After that, you can live like a king in your own house, and when the time is right, you can go public and float your shares in the Stock Exchange, and you will be rich."

The fisherman asks, "And after that?"

The businessman says, "After that, you can finally retire, you can move to a house by the fishing village, wake up early *in the morning, catch a few fish, then return home to play with kids, have a nice afternoon nap with your wife, and when evening comes, you can join your buddies for a drink, play the guitar, sing and dance throughout the night!"*

The fisherman was puzzled, "Isn't that what I am doing now?"

At the age of forty-one at the time of writing this page, I am working full time and now plan to work for as long as my body allows me to (sixty-five or seventy-five may be). That being said, I have slowed down considerably to enjoy life's small pleasures like sitting on the beach and doing nothing, spending time with my son and wife without feeling guilty of not achieving financial targets. I am proud to say that I am living a life I always dreamt of already.

My learning is why postpone what you can enjoy right now.

Every day is a gift…relish it.

Chapter 15

The Spotlight Effect

For a little over two years, I worked for a consulting company managing fortune 500 clients across Australia, New Zealand, and Asia pacific. Consultants are expected to be impeccably dressed, articulate, knowledgeable about client's business and present world class presentation to win over multimillion multiyear deals. In addition, they work sixteen-hour days, live out of a suitcase, get hefty bonuses and a path to partnership but that is not the point of this chapter.

It is a warmest Tuesday of December in Sydney, and I am dressed in a new blue suit, white shirt and a black tie which is like a uniform for consultants as I rush to the domestic terminal of Sydney Airport at 4 am to catch a 5 am flight to Brisbane. It is my fifth visit to the same banking client in as many weeks to meet with all influential stakeholders and multiple dinners in almost all famous restaurants Brisbane has to offer.

Today is the most important visit wherein I am supposed to present the final proposal to win a twelve-million-dollar piece of consulting work spanning over eighteen months. As a high performer and on a partner track, I take this task to heart and put in a tremendous effort over last few months to successfully sign this deal. I have spent countless hours on the presentation, assembling data, analysing trends, cost optimising ideas with targets and priced the deal aggressively to fend off any competition which was circling from all corners.

Over the last week, I have been slightly unwell with ever changing Sydney weather compounded by lack of sleep, continuous travel and almost eighty-hour work weeks for months on end.

Traffic situation at the final intersection of Sydney Domestic Airport can be brutal at this hour depending on the flight schedule and my Uber driver is almost convinced that I am track of missing my 5 am flight today. Luckily, I had booked flexible flight and managed to change my flight to five thirty am through the app and complete the web check-in taking advantage of my platinum mile frequent flyer status.

The flight was on time and I somehow managed to reach client office ten minutes ahead of our nine am meeting surviving long Uber queue at Brisbane airport and bumper to bumper traffic at Brisbane central business district. In the flurry of my early morning, I skipped by breakfast and was surviving on double expresso coffees. As I enter the boardroom and set up my presentation, sharp at nine am, the senior executives walked in expecting me to modernize and revolutionize their business with a magic wand almost instantly.

During my one-hour presentation, while I was presenting, I noticed that I slipped my tongue a couple times on the most crucial PowerPoint slides, to add t my misery I spilled my coffee on the gigantic glass table and almost yawned when I was asked a critical question by the Chief Financial Officer. Finally, the meeting ended, and the senior executives hurried for their ten am meeting even before I had a chance to seek feedback on the presentation and discuss the next steps.

I locked myself in the bathroom, thinking that maybe I am not up to the demands of this role and have no right to be in this aggressive role and on a path of partnership and I just wished if I can turn back time somehow. My anxiety gave way to stomach-ache and almost felt like throwing up. Next day, I managed to have a meeting with my primary contact who was present during the meeting, and he provided great reviews of my presentation and management team was assured of my business knowledge, ability to address their concerns and my consulting company was one of the two shortlisted to win a deal within the next fortnight.

Later that evening during my flight back to Sydney, I realised what I felt was the quintessential Spotlight Effect, where we tend to believe that everyone in the crowd is not only rerunning our mess-up over and over but also thinking that we are a terrible public speaker across the board. And because of it, we assume they must also think we are awful at everything else in life.

We believe we live in our prime-time television show with the spotlight always on us. But the reality is this: we're usually too blinded by our spotlight to stare at anyone else's.

Now, let's examine the same Spotlight Effect in our personal lives, let's say you go to a party at your friend's house, and you are wearing the same black linen shirt with blue denims that you wore in the last get together with similar crowd. Most people will assume that others will instinctively notice the repetition of their attire and judge them over it, in reality other people are more conscious about their own looks, hair, dress, shoes etc.

Your freedom begins the day you realise nobody is thinking about you.

My learnings

1. Recognise that you are not the centre of attraction for everyone you meet. Other people are equally or probably more concerned about what you think about them or judge them. You are always not on the stage; this should take the pressure off.

2. Be content acknowledging that how others judge you in about them and not you.

Chapter 16

Serendipity

My parents have had a great influence in my growing up years and I credit them for keeping me humble and grounded all the time. Family values, living within your means, importance of food & nutrition, trust in God and power of karma have been embedded in our family deeply. Unfortunately, being risk averse is also a virtue I picked up from my family for which I have blame them unfairly at different stages of my life.

I have grown up hearing stories and anecdotes about the role luck plays in our lives and *what is meant to happen always finds a way*. I never believed in the fact that its sensible to leave important things or decisions in your life at the mercy of luck. Instead, my learning so far taught me that one makes his or her own luck and relentless hard work and commitment is all it takes to succeed in life.

As I matured and my life enriched me with more experiences in personal and professional life, I gradually but slowly started appreciating the wisdom in the power of serendipitous meetings, incidents, and people in our lives. Though, I have had several serendipitous moments in my life, let me illustrate a few significant ones.

Meeting my wife

I started my professional journey fairly early with some initial retail and contact centre jobs until 2003 when I landed my first proper corporate job working for a financial services company in New Delhi, India.

It is 4th November 2003, the day I am supposed to be in Bangalore for an official training which gets postponed. Since I am not supposed to be in office that day, I decide to take a day off and just rest up and catch-up with my friends and watch a movie instead. For reasons unknown yet, I finally decide against taking a day off and drive to my office in New Delhi to resume work instead. I park my car in a dusty parking lot in the busy business district of Nehru Place and take the stairs to my first-floor office.

Around noon as I take a break for a quick coffee and head downstairs. As I walk towards the lift, I see a beautiful girl dressed casually in blue denims, flowery colourful casual top, big golden earring, and a big colourful sling bag enough to fit my entire wardrobe. The moment I lay my eyes on this gorgeous creature, I feel a lightning bolt to my heart where I could not think or eat and just run off and get married. Later, I find out that she is visiting my office just for a few hours as a part of her university internship.

I would prefer to keep my story of "how I met my wife" a closely guarded secret not because my wonderful wife would want me to but because it's not that juicy a story. Long story short, after dating for approximately ten years out of which more than half of them were long distant, we got married and I cannot imagine my life with anyone else but her.

Something that has never been lost on me is the fact that I met or saw my future wife on the day I was not supposed to be at work…scratch that, I was not supposed to be in the same city. What would you refer to a fact that my official trip got cancelled and my alternate plan of taking a day off never eventuated? In a massive corporate office wherein it's not uncommon to not see a colleague or even your manager for an entire day, I happened to take a coffee break at an exact moment when this gorgeous girl was standing near the gate fiddling with her phone. If this is not serendipity, I do not know what is?

Landing my first job in a new country

In the year 2015, me and wife made one of the most important decisions of our lives. After establishing ourselves in the corporate life, we both had reached comfortable positions and making substantial money to lead more than comfortable lives.

We are settled in Mumbai, bought, and furnished our dream house. However, both of us had a desire to settle abroad, after my adventurous official trip to Australia in the year 2013, we decide to apply for a permanent residency of the country. Normal life took over and we forgot about our permanent residency application and suddenly on an early October morning, we received a call confirming we have secured our permanent residency of Australia based on our skills and experience.

We are both delighted and yet nervous about it at the same time, imagining that we will end up leaving everything we have worked out for years and start our lives afresh from the very beginning. To add to this, we had not communicated our plans to the families yet.

I land in Sydney; Australia in May and the winter is making its presence felt and we settle in a bread & breakfast accommodation at a beautiful suburb close to the railway station to ensure an easy commute to the city. Luckily for us, my wife lands a decent paying contract job in a large bank within a couple of weeks. For me, the journey of applying to countless jobs was frustrating and demoralizing with more than twenty versions of my resume & cover letter matching individual jobs I shortlisted.

My last job in India was Senior Vice President of a large financial services company and I was managing a team of more than eighty employees. Fortunately, after weeks of cold calling and applying for jobs online, I get a meeting with one of the largest recruitment companies in Australia. I am dressed to impress in a corporate suit and reach thirty minutes ahead of the scheduled meeting. During the meeting, the recruiter discusses my experience, qualification, residency status and specifics roles I would like to apply for. At the end of the meeting, he casually mentions to me that that your resume commands to be shortlisted for a General Manager role, but your lack of Australian experience is hindering your chances of even being shortlisted.

Sensing my confusion, he patiently guides me to restructure my resume and trim significant parts of my experience and target a project manager or operations manager level roles to at least open the interview doors.

Fast forward hundred days of frustration of not being able to land any jobs, I start applying for casual jobs in restaurants, gas stations, department stores etc but to my bad luck, even that entry level minimum paying jobs also required some sort of local experience. By this time, I have had nineteen interviews for eleven different jobs, and I had almost made it to two of these. However, one of the roles got filled internally at the last moment and the other job was put on hold due to cost cutting pressures internally. Recruiters of both these roles apologised to me and offered me luck for my job search.

It is a winter day of October and I dress up in my job-hunting suit and wait in queue at Centrelink office in the city to register for unemployment benefit. I deliberate not carrying my bag filled with multiple copies of my resume and cover letter but my somehow end of carrying it on my shoulders out of habit.

Though there is a Centrelink office close to our house, but I am not sure why I decide to travel to Parramatta CBD instead. It is 8:45 am and the Centrelink office opens at 9 am, having 15 minutes to kill, I enter a large building within the complex to grab a quick cup of coffee. The café is crowded, and a young girl walks up to me and guides me to another café inside the building with $2 voucher to redeem as an introductory offer.

I walk to the other café in search of a hot cup of latte with a $2 voucher. Ten meters before the café, a man dressed casually in denims and a polo t-shirt guides me to the first floor of the building assuming I am here for an interview. He hands me a pamphlet mentioning:

Interview for the following roles

1. **Transformation Manager &**

2. **Process Improvement Lead**

Press 2 to speak to the Human Resource Coordinator and mention the role you have been shortlisted for.

I see a white intercom on the wall and press 2, I mention my name and before I could say anything else, she buzzes me inside. I enter the door and the room has nine chairs neatly organised and within five minutes a lady name Natalie walks up to me and I introduce myself and hand-over a copy of my resume. And just like that my interview starts with a written test with two real life case studies to be solved with detailed steps.

I complete the case study and submit my sheet; in the meantime, I research about the company on my phone. It turns out that I had cracked an interview with one the oldest and largest wealth management companies of Australia & New Zealand. I quickly research about average market salaries of both the roles. With next ten minutes, I was called in for an interview meeting with a panel and I confidently answer their questions. After the interview, Natalie comes back and congratulates me on securing the role pending the background checks.

And just like that I got my first job, I pinch myself multiple times to ensure its real and it takes me a few hours to believe it.

Now just imagine,

Was it a pure coincidence that I go to a faraway Centrelink office dressed in a suit carrying my documents?

Is it not serendipity that the first café was packed, and a lure of $2 voucher makes me try a new unknown café where someone mistakes me of being pre shortlisted for the jobs for which the interviews are being held precisely at that time?

Incidentally some world changing discoveries have been a result of serendipity, my Favorite one is the birth of Penicillin as the story goes:

The discovery of penicillin, one of the world's first antibiotics, marks a true turning point in human history — when doctors finally had a tool that could. completely cure their patients of deadly infectious diseases. Many school children can recite the basics. Penicillin was discovered in London. in September of 1928. As the story goes, Dr. Alexander Fleming, the bacteriologist on duty at St. Mary's Hospital, returned from a summer vacation. in Scotland to find a messy lab bench and a good deal more. Upon examining some colonies of Staphylococcus aureus, Dr. Fleming noted that a Mold called Penicillium notatum had contaminated his Petri dishes. After carefully placing the dishes under his microscope, he was amazed to find that the Mold prevented the normal growth of the staphylococci.

It took Fleming a few more weeks to grow enough of the pernickety Mold so that he was able to confirm his findings. His conclusions turned out to be phenomenal: there was some factor in the Penicillium Mold that not only inhibited the growth of the bacteria but, more important, might be harnessed to combat infectious diseases.

As Dr. Fleming famously wrote about that red-letter date: "When I woke up just after dawn on September 28, 1928, I certainly didn't plan to revolutionize all medicine by discovering the world's first antibiotic, or bacteria killer. But I guess that was exactly what I did."

Chapter 17

Data, Damned lies, Statistics & Correlations (not causation)

When you work in consulting, you get thrown into varied projects to ensure as a resource (yes, you are a resource to generate money for partners) you are billed to a client at least 90% to 95% of your available hours. I had an opportunity to work on projects which I had zero experience in. My background has been strategy, transformation, and process & project management, I got thrown into projects across data analytics, non-financial risk, credit risk and Audit.

The only great thing about working in consulting (if you can survive 16-hour days, billability pressures, new business generation and client & partner tantrums) is that it forces you to learn on the fly and it improves your presentation and stakeholder management skills. You are supposed to know the client systems, processes, business, gaps, strategy better than their employees from day one since they are paying you top dollars on hourly basis.

In preparation of starting a data analytics project for a financial service client based in New Zealand, I attended a one-day course in big data in Auckland, New Zealand.

The course helped me a great deal to understand basis of different tools like SAS, R, and Python but the final module titled "causation & correlation" stunned me completely. Let me illustrate:

The faculty from a renowned New Zealand University dressed in a casual jacket highlights a slide titled: "When can data lie?" on slide 1. With stunned silence across eighty attendees, he clicks the cursor, and the word "always" appears in bold. He continues with some real-life examples where data can be manipulated depends on the desired result. Then he asks an open question to the audience comprising of financial services industry largely.

"What is the best predictor of the returns on S&P 500 index?"

Varied answers are shouted by the tired audience namely:

1. Interest rates

2. Bond Yields

3. GDP growth

4. Earnings

5. Trade deficit

6. Geopolitical tensions

7. Regulations

The faculty moves across the stage with a poker face and clicks on next slide that mentions:

Butter Production in Bangladesh

Butter production in Bangladesh had the tightest correlation to the S&P 500 to any other data series ever analysed.

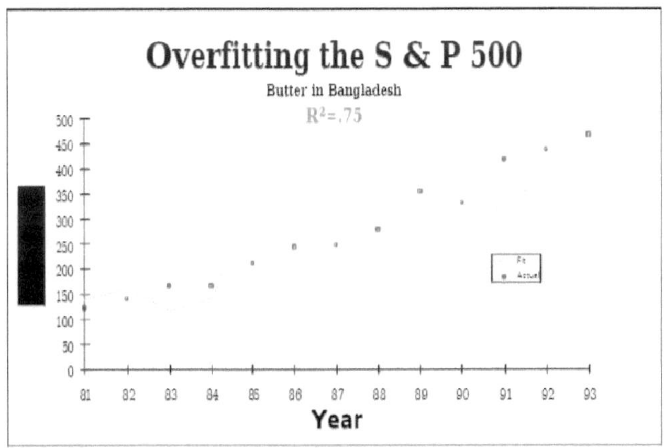

Obviously increase in butter production in Bangladesh does not cause S&P 500 index to jump and vice versa, the key take aways are:

1. Correlation does not mean causation.

2. Data can be manipulated to suit an insight or theory.

3. Beware of fancy statistics before making a significant decision

Another general example of causation Vs correlation is:

Ice cream causes people to buy sunscreen

1. When people buy ice cream, the sales of sunscreen goes up.

2. Therefore eating ice cream causes people to buy sunscreen.

You can probably figure out why this is wrong. Ice cream doesn't make people buy sunscreen. But sunscreen doesn't make people buy ice cream either. It's also not a complete random coincidence - there is a correlation here. Instead, when it's hot and sunny outside, people like to eat ice cream and buy sunscreen. However, notice that neither the sun, nor the hot temperature are mentioned anywhere in this:

This is an example of someone not noticing that the cause is elsewhere. The two things they are looking at - ice cream and sunscreen - are correlated, but the cause is something entirely different - the hot weather and the sun!

No wonder while making significant decisions about business, Jeff Bezos says "when the anecdotes and the data disagree, the anecdotes are usually right. There is something wrong with the way you are measuring it.

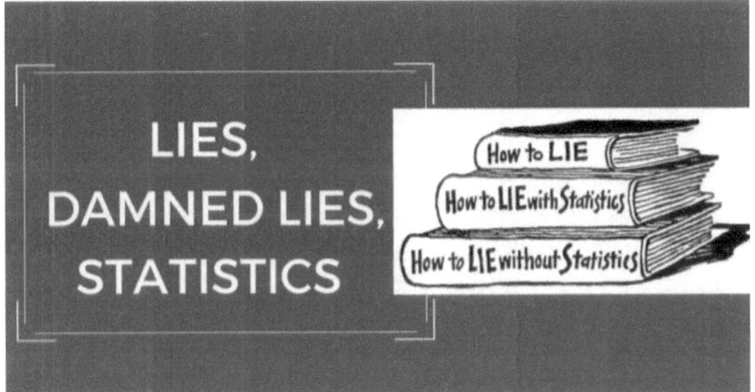

Chapter 18

Fame and Dreams

Becoming famous is amazing. - Being famous is a mixed bag. - Losing fame is miserable............... Will Smith

If you are born in India, the chances are you have dreamed of becoming a cricketer or a movie star (though your parents would insist on becoming a doctor and an engineer) and achieve a level of fame very few people in the world have experienced. Believe me when I say this "Michael Jordan or Tom Hanks has no idea of the stardom bestowed upon Sachin Tendulkar or Shahrukh Khan". When a billion people love you, they treat you God like.

I was no different growing up, fortunately I realised early in life that I have no skill or looks to be an actor. I had stage fright and hence I never even participated in a school play so facing a real camera was out of question. However, I was a great cricket player as an opening batsman, occasional medium pace bowler and a captain of my school team and local club team for years.

When I failed to make it to my state team (Ranji Trophy), I gave up my unrealistic dream of becoming a cricketer and joined my first part time job and never looked back. There has always been a tinge of regret when I see the kind of adulation star cricketers enjoy and not to dismiss the millions of dollars, they make from endorsement alone across the world. Now, I believe actors and sport persons deserve every ounce of fame and dollars they make for their hard work and commitment of their craft and not to mention lack of privacy in the age of paparazzi, social media, and camera phones.

There are few celebrities like Mahindra Singh Dhoni (ex-Indian cricket captain who won 2 world cups (T20 and One day) and Matthew Perry (Chandler Bing of friends who needs no introduction). Having read or watched almost all celebrity memoirs & biographies or (biographical) movies, the recent book my Matthew Perry has had a deep impact on me – part of the reason could be that he is my favourite actor as well. I sincerely recommend reading his book titled "friends, lovers and the big terrible things" in which he unapologetically describes the pain he faced throughout his life in spite of being one of the most recognisable celebrities in the world and at the heights of "Friends" making more than a million dollars per episode and of course dating Julia Roberts.

Matthew Perry has spent almost all his life chasing fame and overcoming his fear of being an "unaccompanied minor" due to lack of attention and love he received from his parents and family. His life is one of both privilege and pain. Born into a wealthy family and blessed with talent and charisma, he achieved overnight success on the hit sitcom Friends. Yet behind the scenes, Perry struggled with a deep-seated addiction that threatened to destroy his life.

Matthew describes that fame can be a double-edged sword. On the one hand, it can bring wealth, success, and popularity. On the other hand, it can also lead to isolation, loneliness, and substance abuse.

Matthew Perry writes about how he struggled with isolation and loneliness after becoming famous. He felt surrounded by people who were only interested in him for his fame and money. This made him feel like he couldn't trust anyone.

For example, Perry describes how he would often go to parties and events, but he would feel like he was on display rather than enjoying himself. He also describes how he would often be approached by people who only wanted to talk about his work or ask him for autographs. This made Perry feel like he wasn't being seen as a person, but rather as a celebrity.

Perry's isolation and loneliness led him to turn to drugs and alcohol to cope. He writes about how he would drink heavily to numb his feelings and to feel more confident in social situations. However, Perry's drinking only made his isolation and loneliness worse. He began to push away his friends and family, and he became more and more dependent on drugs and alcohol.

Perry's life is a reminder that fame does not protect people from isolation, loneliness, and addiction. In fact, these problems can be even more acute for celebrities, who are often surrounded by people who are not genuinely interested in them.

Few quotes from his memoir moved me and brough tears to my eyes:

"I think you actually have to have all of your dreams come true to realize they are the wrong dreams."

"It is very odd to live in a world where if you died, it would shock people but surprise no one."

"Do you know what St. Peter says to everyone who tries to get into heaven? … Peter says, 'Don't you have any scars?' And when most would respond proudly, 'Well, no, no I don't,' Peter says, 'Why not? Was there nothing worth fighting for?"

"The man takes the drink; the drink takes all the rest."

"You never know where one thing will lead… I guess the lesson is, take every opportunity, because something might come of it."

"And have you ever stood on the water's edge and tried to stop the wave? It goes on regardless of what we do, regardless of how hard we try. The ocean reminds us that we are powerless in comparison."

"Now, all these years later, I'm certain that I got famous so I would not waste my entire life trying to get famous. You have to get famous to know that it's not the answer. And nobody who is not famous will ever truly believe that."

Chapter 19

Experiences, Scars, and disagreements

My Dad has played a pivotal role in my life and I have picked up most of his virtues like financial management, family values and hard work among others. During my adulthood, when I was old enough to build my virtues and personality, I often had disagreement with my dad's resistance to not spend any money on himself. He would spend freely during family dinners, shopping for me and my siblings, entertaining guests and maintaining our home with new comforts & gadgets but categorically refuse to replace his worn-out shoes or his visibly frayed shirt.

During early 2013, my dad had completed almost all his financial commitments like:

1. Me and my sibling's education of our choice

2. Paid for all 3 lavish weddings of all 3 kids.

3. Owned a decent business and a house in an affluential suburb.

4. He was debt free.

5. He a healthy combination of investments, savings, and health insurance.

As I started earning and spending at ease, I began to seriously wonder the deep potential causes that led my dad to almost never spend on himself. He only vice was a nice dinner as a family as and when possible and to this date, he would never let anyone of us pay for those dinners. To this date, he is against taking any loans and advocates to live within our means, to an extent he contributed significantly to pay off my mortgage. I often thought about this and asked myself, "will I become a version of him at his age", most of the time my answer was NO because I always envisioned myself to spend lavishly post-retirement.

When probed about this, one of his pet phrases translated in English is "we have had to tie a knot to every cent to make it a dollar one day" and hence it is impossible for me to spend on unnecessary luxuries for myself.

It is a simple case of generational gap we keep hearing about, after years of analysis, I finally cracked it recently. His childhood experience of lack of basics have left a scar so deep that he finds frivolous expenses repelling.

Let me briefly illustrate his childhood and upbringing. My grandfather was a wealthy merchant with massive family and fortune. The partition of India during 1947 meant that he had to leave everything and migrate to New Delhi with bare essentials, wife and 3 kids and start his life afresh with almost nothing. Though my dad was born in Delhi in 1956 and did not experience the barbaric acts of the partition, he did experience the after-effects of it. There was barely enough food and money for fancy shoes and clothes was almost unthinkable. Seventy-five years of partition have passed but those scars ensured a lifelong commitment to save as much because future can be uncertain.

I have had a privileged life and though the thought of those atrocities during partition of 1947 still make my blood boil and what our previous generation experienced is beyond something we cannot fathom. This leads me to the following question?

- How would I behave if my experiences were different?

- What would me my outlook to money if I was born in 1940's or 1950's?

- Do most disagreements occur due to people with different experiences explaining their point of view?

I have another real-life story to share to illustrate differences due to experiences and previous scars leading to disagreements, this time in corporate life.

My cousin who is a Stanford graduate and about a decade younger than me is a techie based in Silicon Valley and has made it big financially. His first start up which he bootstrapped with a friend was acquired by a massive investor for approximately US $78 million in 2016 of which his share was split into half cash and half equity in the company with a two-year sunset period ensuring non-compete clause.

His mentor and ex professor played a pivotal role in the securing the deal with multiple rounds of negotiation, due diligence, legalities and paperwork. He had an unbreakable trust in his mentor, and he would follow his advice blindly. After his non-compete period was over, he incorporates another company this time in equal partnership with his mentor, a fact that he was immensely proud of and within next fourteen months built a unique prototype product which had massive potential. Due to sensitive nature of the product and the ecosystem they operate it, unfortunately I am not at a liberty of sharing the specifics.

I had an opportunity to visit California recently to catch up with my cousin, this trip had to be postponed twice due a Covid-19 during which flying became a distant dream.

I land at San Francisco airport at 7 am after a 14-hour direct flight from Sydney and my cousin was there to pick me up in his Porshe 911 convertible with barely enough space to accommodate my small bags. We raced through his pacific heights 11-bedroom, 10-bathroom $21 million dollar mansion with a tennis court and

2 swimming pool fitted with Steam and Sauna rooms within 25 minutes. There was hardly any traffic at this time, and I silently felt jealous of his wealth, his mansion had 7 coffee machines installed strategically to ensure a caffeine shot is accessible from any corner of his massive abode.

As I settled in a lavish room on first floor with a mesmerizing view of the mountains, he excused himself to attend a quick Zoom meeting and promised to catch-up for a breakfast at 9 am. I take a quick hot shower resisting the temptation of a Jacuzzi for two installed in the bathroom with an uninterrupted view of his tennis court through a borderless glass wall.

With our respective lattes in hand made from one of his vast collections of coffee machines, we discussed some family gossip and reminisced on our childhood. In deep thought, he said "I wish we could go back to our childhood and never grow up", I was baffled with what I heard and thought to myself, who would not be happy with his fortune. I could retire if I just had this house, forget the tens of millions of dollars of his net worth.

Sensing his stress, I asked him brother I am sure something is bothering you deeply, you can either beat around the bush and hesitate or else come to the point and let me know why you were so eager for me to take this trip apart from showing off your massive wealth and I chuckled.

He opens up and says, look we have built a successful prototype of a product which is significantly ahead than anyone has ever built and there is a massive potential across the world for it. Both me and my partner are sure that can ink our names in history by commercialising this and we have already received considerable interest from Europe, China, and the rest of Asia. We are witnessing some hostile takeover attempts by the competitors, and we have survived only because we are not a public company yet and majority of the investment is internal.

Failing to spot a problem, I interrupt by saying, brother this all sounds great, and I am not surprised with our new success. I know how hard you have worked, and your passion has kept you so busy that you are not yet married, the fact that your mother wanted me to discuss with you seriously with a couple of potential matches based right here in California.

He clearly ignores my marriage jibe and comes straight to the point and says to commercialise our product at scale we desire, we need the following:

1. An external investment of upwards of $200 million

2. Approximately 150 software engineers and testers in United States alone which are almost impossible to hire in California if you are not Google, Amazon, Netflix or Tesla

3. Ability to withstand competition from massive corporations who can undercut you every step of the way.

I have had a few discussions with venture capitalists who have shown interest in investing in scaling up the venture and support our hiring efforts, the biggest challenge is that my partner and mentor want us to either licence our product or sell it and cash in our chips. I wish to put all my chips back on the table even if I had to sell my house to make it happen and decide to terminate the partnership and go alone in the venture.

I realised that I am not skilled or experienced enough in entrepreneurship and or business to offer any expert advice and therefore all I did is give him a patient ear, I knew this is something he cannot discuss openly with too many people. He impromptu decides to host a barbeque and pizza dinner with a few of his close friends including his partner, he sends a few texts, and it was organised for 7 pm.

We played a few tennis sets and I realised that I knees are nowhere agile and strong as they were last time I held a tennis racquet. We talked some more, took a dip in the pool and ended the afternoon with a sauna session to relax my muscles.

We both get ready and almost all his invitees reached on time and I admired their sense of punctuality and thought to myself, may be that's a secret sauce to success in bay area apart from being visionary and a risk taker.

I had an opportunity to have long conversations with the few guests and I picked up a few traits of entrepreneurship, so I thought and hoped actually.

We had awesome shrimps and steak on barbeque and at least 20 pizzas between 7 people freshly made in wood fired oven placed a few meters away from the main swimming pool on ground floor. In so many ways, this was a perfect party digression I needed after covid 19 and the party finished few minutes post mid-night. With guests departing and my jetlag beginning to make its presence felt, I decide to call it a night and crashed in my room on first floor.

Next day, I wake up at 9:30 am and saw my cousin impeccable dressed and on a Zoom call with at least 20 other attendees across the world. I was thoroughly impressed with his professionalism, I let him finish his work and drown myself in a difficult to resist Jacuzzi with an extra hot latte.

During that afternoon, we both take a walk in the beautiful neighborhood and while admiring the magnificent mansions with massive boundary walls and immaculate gardens, I decide to take the discussion to his professional venture. I begin by saying, brother have you tried exploring the potential reason/s to understand why your mentor and partner on whom you will trust your life with wants to opt for a different approach?

He said, the only reason is that he is old and risk averse and probably wants to retire without understanding that I am young and wants to be in it to win it. I decide to share my detailed conversation over multiple old-fashioned cocktails with his partner last night. I say from my conversations with him, my understanding is that during the dot-com bubble of the year 2000, he was in the similar position, he lost his fortune by ignoring the $11 million offer he had from an IT company and decided to go all in.

Next 2 years saw bloodbath on wall street and he lost nearly all of it and had to file for chapter 7 of the bankruptcy act here in United States and went back to teach at Stanford.

The scar of dot-com bubble is the reason, he is afraid that if you both decide to go all in, either of the following could eventuate:

1. You both will need to liquidate majority of your stakes to raise funds thereby losing your majority voting rights to institutional investors.

2. Even if you succeed in hiring massive numbers of talented professionals, big corporates with unlimited cash will end up offering more and taking them away.

3. You will lose your early mover advantage and competition from other players will reduce your unique value proposition.

I continue by saying, since you are fortunate enough to not experience the dot-com bubble, maybe you are oblivious to certain potential challenges and realities of playing and competing with the big corporates who will do whatever in their limitless power to crush you.

Long story short, he had a heart felt discussion with his partner and they both understood their unique perspective which makes it easy to jointly decide the way forward.

That evening, I finally realised my dream to drive a 1956 red Ford Mustang convertible on Golden Gate bridge during our trip to Twin Peaks.

Chapter 20

Focus on what Truly Matters

School life for me has been the most special part of my life and I strongly believe the friends you make in school are precious because you have actually grown up with them and there is not much to pretend or judge. I also feel lucky that my schooling happened before the advent of social media and unnecessary technology that has dominated the lives of kids these days. We made real connections and have memorable stories with our friends that can bring a smile to my face.

Please do not get me wrong, technology has been a massive enabler for all of us to stay connected with each other over the years, especially when most of my school friends relocated overseas. We generally get an opportunity to catch-up at least once a year but thanks to our school who hosted an alumni event for our batch in 2023, most of us from all over the world got together and reminisced.

The alumni meet was scheduled on 4th February in the school premises, an opportunity to wander around the school campus after more than 2 decades filled me with excitement. Memories of having fun on the corridors, getting punished, bunking classes and teasing each other dominated my mind and bring a smile to my face as I landed in New Delhi a couple of days before.

Our most beloved teacher in school used to be Mr Sharma who knew an art of mixing fun with studies and occasionally taught us great life's lessons and wisdom along the way. Most of my batch mates including myself were in regular touch with him through WhatsApp and zoom calls. He was gracious enough to invite all of us for a casual coffee to his home on 3rd February at 5 pm and almost everyone RSVP'd yes for the event instantaneously.

It is an unusually cold late afternoon when gradually everyone starts to arrive at Mr Sharma's residence, he greets everyone with excitement and enthusiasm and looks perfectly healthy and fit for his age. Barring is rapidly greying hair and few visible wrinkles on his face, he has not changed much. I am meeting few of my friends after more than ten years and could feel the age taking its toll on almost all of us physically.

We gather in his living room and by 5:20 pm, all of us had an opportunity to catch-up with each other and share the latest in our lives. It's a massive room with an old but modern sofa at the centre of the room with a relatively small glass coffee table. The walls are filled with family pictures in neat frames and assorted chairs surrounding the sofa to accommodate approximately twenty-two guests.

Mr Sharma stands in front of the room and mentions how delighted he is to see and host all of us and an impromptu two-way conversation kick in enthusiastically which soon took a sombre turn. Most of us start to complaint about the general pressures of professional lives coupled with responsibilities of expanded families and remiss on an amazing school life where the only pressure was to do well during exams.

Some of us decide to show off their wealth through pictures of their mansions, luxury cars and home theatres etc but a common theme of stress, pressure and lack of time dominated the discussion. Mr Sharma on the contrary focusses on stories about his two boys and their modest holidays, his simple house and importance of healthy eating habits and sports. He is still enjoying the same job of teaching business studies to year 11 and 12 and inculcate a sense of simplicity in their lives.

Offering all of us coffee, he goes to his kitchen and returns with a variety of mugs and a massive pot of homemade coffee and instructs us to help ourselves. We were amazed to see a variety of plastic, glass, crystal, new and old coffee mugs neatly placed on the table with no specific order.

When we all had a cup of coffee in hand, the professor said: "If you noticed, all the nice-looking expensive cups were taken up first up, leaving behind the plain and cheap ones. While it is but normal for you to want only the best for yourselves, that is the source of your problems and stress generally. "The cup itself doesn't add to the quality or the taste of the coffee and in some cases even hides what we drink and yet you consciously went for the best-looking cups."

Then, we began eyeing each other's cups.

With compassion, he added, "Life is like coffee. The jobs, money and position in society are the cups. They are just tools to hold and contain Life, and the type of cup we have does not define, nor change the quality of Life we live. While you pursue the fine cups, be sure to keep focus on enjoying the coffee!"

I could not help but wonder which all worries or priorities are actually like a cup and does not add much to the coffee.

Let me share with you another life altering experience which altered my perspective on value of focus and its impact on results.

Sometime last year, we were invited for dinner by our friends who live in the neighbourhood and me and my wife were looking forward to the evening hoping for a welcome change from diapers and incessant screaming of my one-year-old son. Luckily, two more families with kids are joining us for the get together and kids can play or may be watch television for some time giving all the tired parents some much needed peace and rest.

The hosts had a magnificent Victorian-style mansion with a grand facade adorned with intricate details and ornate architecture. Its sprawling grounds were meticulously landscaped, featuring vibrant flower gardens, manicured lawns, and serene ponds. The exterior of the house was painted in soft pastel colours, adding to its inviting and tranquil ambience.

Inside, the house was just as breathtaking. The interior was tastefully decorated with luxurious furnishings, elegant chandeliers, and exquisite artwork adorning the walls. Each room was thoughtfully designed with attention to detail, creating a sense of warmth and opulence throughout the house.

On the outside, adjacent to a rectangle pool, they had installed a wood fired pizza oven which was to be inaugurated today. Each guest had an opportunity to pick their own toppings amongst the freshly chopped mushrooms, tomatoes, pineapples, artichokes, Spanish onion, corn and endless varieties of pepperoni and chicken were neatly placed on a table.

While enjoying scrumptious pizzas with chilled pacific ale, one of the parents initiated an interesting challenge they are facing with their eldest daughter named Eva who is in eighth standard.

She describes "Eva is brilliant in physics and almost always at ninety fifth percentile in her school, but she is struggling in Mathematics where she scores around fifty-two percentiles". The parents have tried varies ways of motivating Eva to focus more on math and improve, additional tuitions classes have not helped either.

Another parent intervened and asked, "why don't you let her focus on excelling and be the best physicist she can become rather than focussing on a subject she is not much interested in"? He further added "look if she focusses too much on improving a subject that she is not very good or interested in, the best she would become is an average". However, if you encourage her to focus on physics which clearly she loves and doing well in, she can be extra ordinary and the best in her field.

It did not take much time for me to understand the deep wisdom in what I just heard but since I had no experience in raising school kids, I decided not to contribute to the discussion. I quickly decide that I would let my son chose his Favorite subjects and encourage him to be the best in his chosen field than be average in multiple fields.

This discussion reminded me on a quote I read somewhere which I always try and use in my professional life:

"Focus on your strengths, hire for weakness".

Chapter 21

Patience as a Virtue

*"Patience is when you are supposed to get mad,
but you choose to understand".*

One of my long-cherished dreams is to learn to play drums and I have successfully convinced myself for last 12 years that this is not the right time to spend money and time on hobbies. I often dream of myself being a part of a band and performing live shows and the audiences are loving every beat.

In early 2017, I finally gathered courage to enrol myself to learn playing drums and I was lucky enough to get a coach who worked on creating a foundation for me. From the beginning, he made me focussed on basics like learning to "read the notes" and he said if you can read the notes perfectly, you can learn to play any instrument in the world. However, my patience got the best of me because the music academy was hosting a show to provide a platform for the students in the next two months and

I had mentally selected myself to be a lead drummer for the gig.

Irritated by lack of patience, my coach introduced to the following story which changed the way I looked at events on my life.

Once there was an old man who lived in a tiny village. Although poor, he was envied by all, for he owned a beautiful white horse. Even the king coveted his treasure. A horse like this had never been seen before—such was its splendour, its majesty, its strength.

People offered fabulous prices for the steed, but the old man always refused. "This horse is not a horse to me," he would tell them. "It is a person. How could you sell a person? He is a friend, not a possession. How could you sell a friend?" The man was poor, and the temptation was great. But he never sold the horse.

One morning he found that the horse was not in the stable. All the village came to see him. "You old fool," they scoffed, "we told you that someone would steal your horse. We warned you that you would be robbed. You are so poor. How could you ever hope to protect such a valuable animal? It would have been better to have sold him. You could have gotten whatever price you wanted. No amount would have been too high. Now the horse is gone, and you've been cursed with misfortune."

The old man responded, "Don't speak too quickly. Say only that the horse is not in the stable. That is all we know; the rest is judgment. If I've been cursed or not, how can you know? How can you judge?"

The people contested, "Don't make us out to be fools! We may not be philosophers, but great philosophy is not needed. The simple fact that your horse is gone is a curse."

The old man spoke again. "All I know is that the stable is empty, and the horse is gone. The rest I don't know. Whether it be a curse or a blessing, I can't say. All we can see is a fragment. Who can say what will come next?"

The people of the village laughed. They thought that the man was crazy. They had always thought he was a fool; if he wasn't, he would have sold the horse and lived off the money. But instead, he was a poor woodcutter, an old man still cutting firewood and dragging it out of the forest and selling it. He lived hand to mouth in the misery of poverty. Now he had proven that he was, indeed, a fool.

After fifteen days, the horse returned. He hadn't been stolen; he had run away into the forest. Not only had he returned, but he had also brought a dozen wild horses with him. Once again, the village people gathered around the woodcutter and spoke. "Old man, you were right, and we were wrong. What we thought was a curse was a blessing. Please forgive us."

The man responded, "Once again, you go too far. Say only that the horse is back. State only that a dozen horses returned with him, but don't judge. How do you know if this is a blessing or not? You see only a fragment. Unless you know the whole story, how can you judge? You read only one page of a book. Can you judge the whole book? You read only one word of a phrase. Can you understand the entire phrase?

"Life is so vast, yet you judge all of life with one page or one word. All you have is a fragment! Don't say that this is a blessing. No one knows. I am content with what I know. I am not perturbed by what I don't."

"Maybe the old man is right," they said to one another. So, they said little. But down deep, they knew he was wrong. They knew it was a blessing. Twelve wild horses had returned with one horse. With a little bit of work, the animals could be broken and trained and sold for much money.

The old man had a son, an only son. The young man began to break the wild horses. After a few days, he fell from one of the horses and broke both legs. Once again, the villagers gathered around the old man and cast their judgments.

"You were right," they said. "You proved you were right. The dozen horses were not a blessing. They were a curse. Your only son has broken his legs, and now in your old age you have no one to help you. Now you are poorer than ever."

The old man spoke again. "You people are obsessed with judging. Don't go so far. Say only that my son broke his legs. Who knows if it is a blessing or a curse? No one knows. We only have a fragment. Life comes in fragments."

It so happened that a few weeks later the country engaged in war against a neighbouring country. All the young men of the village were required to join the army. Only the son of the old man was excluded, because he was injured. Once again, the people gathered around the old man, crying and screaming because their sons had been taken. There was little chance that they would return. The enemy was strong, and the war would be a losing struggle. They would never see their sons again.

"You were right, old man," they wept. "God knows you were right. This proves it. Yours son's accident was a blessing. His legs may be broken, but at least he is with you. Our sons are gone forever."

The old man spoke again. "It is impossible to talk with you. You always draw conclusions. No one knows. Say only this: Your sons had to go to war, and mine did not. No one knows if it is a blessing or a curse. No one is wise enough to know. Only God knows."

The old man was right. We only have a fragment. Life's mishaps and horrors are only a page out of a grand book. We must be slow about drawing conclusions. We must reserve judgment on life's storms until we know the whole story.

I don't know where the woodcutter learned his patience. Perhaps from another woodcutter in Galilee. For it was the Carpenter who said it best:

"Do not worry about tomorrow, for tomorrow will worry about itself."

Another timeless story which imbibes patience as a virtue:

The Long Taxi Ride Story

One evening, a New York City taxi driver arrived at his last pickup for his shift. After honking and waiting a few minutes, the passenger hadn't come out yet. Because he had had a long day, he considered leaving a few minutes later. Instead, he parked his taxi and went to knock on the door.

He heard an old lady's voice yell, "Just a minute."

A small woman in her 90's eventually answered the door and kindly asked the taxi driver, "Could you carry my bag?"

The cab driver walked the lady and her bags to the cab. Once there, she handed the driver an address and asked if they could drive through downtown.

"It's not the shortest way," The driver answered.

The lady then told him that she wasn't in a hurry, as she was headed to a hospital facility. She said, "I don't have any family left and my doctor says I don't have very long."

The driver then turned off the meter and asked which route she wanted him to take.

For the next two hours, the taxi driver and the lady drove through the city. She had the driver go by her former place of employment, a house where she once lived, and her old dance studio.

There were even some parts of the town where she asked the taxi driver to slow down so she could sit in silence, staring into the darkness.

After a few hours, the lady requested to go to her destination, saying she was tired.

When they arrived at their destination, two nurses came out to the cab to retrieve the lady with a wheelchair.

She asked the driver, "How much do I owe you?"

"Nothing," he responded.

"I must owe you *something*," she persisted.

"There will be other passengers," said the taxi driver.

The driver then bent over and hugged the lady. She whispered to him, "Thank you. You gave an old woman a few more moments of joy."

The driver could hardly speak when he pulled away. What if that woman had gotten an impatient driver? Or someone who refused to get out and pick her up at her door? Or refused to drive around the city?

Hindsight

Be patient in conversation. There may be an important lesson waiting to be learned in your interactions with others.

The woman wasn't the only one to benefit that day, as the cab driver was able to feel the significance of his actions for her, and knowledge of how precious life is.

Take some time to find more patience with the people you interact with, whether that's listening intently to your partner, having a conversation with your kids, or checking in with a friend.

Chapter 22

Incentives & Justification

By Jason Zweig

On a drizzly evening in New York, United States, I am just finishing up my quick run in the Central Park, an iconic place made famous by numerous American movies and series. It's always been my dream to experience a morning and an evening stroll in Central Park. It's around 7 pm and I walk back to my hotel room in Wyndham hotel to have a quick shower and be ready for an 8:30 pm dinner with a friend at Tavern on The Green.

As I head to my hotel through the Manhattan by lanes, a thirty something man dressed in a grey hoodie, blue denims, and worn-out Adidas shoes was walking towards me. We come across each other and I could not help but notice few scars on his face and unkept beard when he asks me "its $100 for a small dose and its pure". I have been warned about pickpockets and drug dealer targeting New York tourists at night but experiencing it firsthand is a strange experience.

I casually ask him, hey mate, do you mind if we had a quick chat and I give him $20, all the cash I had on me to just keep it. He agrees and we stand beneath a shed from where I can see my hotel on the next block, I say, look I don't do drugs and I am not a cop; I am here on a three-day business trip, but can I ask you an honest question? He says shoot bro......I asked do you understand the impact of what you do on vulnerable people and society at large?

He paused, almost seems conscious and says strongly, look man, there is always guilt, but extreme poverty and terminally ill mother will not make you feel the pain of that guilt. I almost felt embarrassed of judging this man and asking an uncomfortable question, I say, I would love to help you land a job to support your family… before I could complete my sentence he shoots back thanks for the offer, I really appreciate it. But I am an undocumented migrant and have been lied, cheated and exploited and offered multiple jobs where I laboured for

16-hour days and without being paid because they all know that I cannot report them or do nothing. Worst, if they report me, I will be jailed and deported.

It suddenly dawns on me that selling coke is easy to justify in your head when you have mouths to feed and sick family members to take care of and to top is all you are living in a country illegally. When you understand how powerful incentives can be, you stop judging people doing things that society does not approve or are looked down upon.

Should we judge media who continue to bombard us with bias story 24/7? We know their incentive is to top viewers ratings and have families to feed in the competitive industry and marketplace.

Think about what in what areas will you act differently if your motivations were to change?

Chapter 23

Simplicity, effort and skill in the age of complexity

"Simplicity is a great virtue, but it
requires hard work to achieve it and education
to appreciate it. And to make matters worse:
complexity sells better."

– Edsger Wybe Dijkstra

I write this chapter sipping a piccolo from the airport lounge of recently renovated Kingsford Smith Airport in Sydney. Usually, I find the aircraft boarding process irritatingly complex specially when one has to verify same document multiple times in separate queues and the process usually takes anywhere from 60 to 90 minutes on a decent day. Holiday and busy season are a different story, and it is not uncommon for airlines to instruct passengers to arrive anywhere between 3 to 4 hours ahead of the scheduled departure time.

Today it's a surprisingly great experience with contact less airline boarding through a kiosk where I was able to quickly input all my passport, trip and destination information. I scan my luggage, and the system printed luggage labels and a slot opens up for me to push my bags into oblivion. From there I move to immigration check counter (this is the most dreadful part of the process with regular delays) which is contact less this time. I scan my passport through a screen, remove my glasses and look at the camera and the screen processes something for a couple of seconds and boom the gate opens and the entire boarding process is complete.

Now that the simple and efficient boarding process has saved me approximately 40 to 60 minutes, I decide to enjoy some coffee and a burrito at the lounge on a massage chair and write this chapter. I just love simplicity and efficiency and have a natural smile on my face.

I have always had a knack of simplifying things throughout my life and therefore I am having a hard time deciding which ones to includes in this chapter.

Let me start with an interesting one:

It is November 2016, I work for a Wealth Management company in Sydney, Australia. Being new to the role, I am observing a solution workshop for a problem or an issue the team is struggling with for years.

Problem Statement – Some of customer requests which are processed offshore in Bangalore, India needs to be sent back Onshore in Sydney since the Offshore team is not authorised to process those transactions. This leads to significant delays and breach of service levels promised to the customers. One of the reasons for delay is time zone difference of +-5.5 hours/+-4.5 hours (depending on daylight saving).

Approximate cost per transaction (Processed in Sydney)- $80

Approximate cost per transaction (processed in Bangalore) - $21

Progress till date – In the last four years, three major projects have been completed which combined resulted in:

1. Shift timings realignment to India and Sydney teams to minimize the time zone difference – resulting in 1.5 hours improvement in service levels.

2. Streamlining of workflow tool with multiple batch jobs during the day

3. Simplifying the procedure document resulting in 6% reduction in requests being transferred back to Onshore team.

Projects cost so far – The above 3 projects have costed the company AUD $568,000 and have failed to deliver tangible improvement in service levels.

Management has allocated a further budget of $250,000 with a non-negotiable target of reducing at least 50% onshore referral within next eight months.

The meeting starts promptly at 9 am and we are sitting in a massive board room overlooking Sydney Harbour bridge and Opera house at a 30-degree angle and I just feel plain lucky to be in the boardroom which is bigger than a normal sized badminton court. There are overall thirteen members in the project team comprising of:

1 Project Manager

2 Business Subject Matter Expert

2 Outsourced team members flown from Bangalore, India

1 Solution Architect

2 Business Analysts

2 Customer Service Starr

1 Risk & Compliance partner

1 Head of Service Delivery (Project Sponsor)

1 Me

We have Pellegrino water (both still & sparkling), apple & orange juice bottles, assorted muffins, cheese platter and a dozen variety of pies to ensure there is no shortage of creativity in the room.

Robin dressed in an impressive blue skirt and a crisp white shirt starts the meeting with a mission statement and says, "we need to make it happen, just tell me directly all you need, but remember we cannot fail this time". Now let's discuss the ideas and potential solutions to achieve 50% reductions in onshore referrals.

Some of the ideas discussed but not limited to were:

1. Create a priority queue to process transactions about to breach service levels – significant system changes required.

2. Redesign end to end procedure and look for wasteful steps.

3. Change promised service levels from current 48 hours to 96 hours.

4. Engage a big 4 consulting company to help and support.

It's almost noon and I can see frustration on Robyn's face, and we are scheduled to break for lunch in the next 12 minutes, I can already see gourmet grilled chicken, Salmon salad, assorted steaks and sandwiches being wheeled in by the pantry staff.

Though I am just paid to observe and learn the ways of working for the company and build stakeholder connections, I have been stopping myself to suggest an idea for the last half an hour. Finally, 10 minutes before the scheduled gourmet lunch, I raise my hand and say, "can I suggest a potential solution"?

I can see stunned faces around the room as if to say something like:

"What does this new guy know about our business?",

"See we have a know it all in the room".

Robyn stands up and encourages me to come towards a massive board and share my idea.

I walk up to the board and a giant screen and repeat few statistics we have discussed over the last 3 hours. I say approximately 34% of the request received by offshore teams are referred Onshore, on an average it creates a delay of 1.6 days. Cost of processing a transaction is one-fourth of the cost of processing in Sydney. None of the projects so far have delivered a tangible improvement.

Considering all this, rather than finding and delivering ways to reduce referral time, why don't we train the offshore teams to process those complex requests and kill the complete onshore referral process itself?

By doing this, we would ensure 100% of customer requests and processed within turnaround time and reduce cost per transaction significantly as an additional benefit.

It's exactly 12 noon and the project manager suggests that we proceed for lunch and "anyways this complex problem cannot have such a simple solution in the first place". Keeping my ego in control, I don't say anything, and Robyn called for lunch, and we are scheduled to be back in the room by 12:45 PM. I take a quick bathroom break, eat 2 massive pieces of salmon followed by a steak sandwich and 2 bottles of apple juice and take a lift downstairs to enjoy a quick walk towards the Opera House to see tourists clicking pictures non-stop.

Its 12:43 pm and everyone has promptly assembled back to the boardroom. Robyn quickly summarises the day so far and with a smile on her face requests all of us to brainstorm the impact of my idea/solution.

Long story short, around 2:10 PM that day, it was unanimously endorsed that we will implement my solution which will not cost anything except for time spent training the offshore team and the project was delivered successfully with 41 days.

Effort Vs Skill

A good friend shared this story recently; a nice story about effort vs. skill – a good reminder that in many areas of work/life time and outcome aren't always aligned; especially in the design & technology space…

A giant ship's engine failed. The ship's owners tried one 'professional' after another but none of them could figure out how to fix the broken engine.

Then they brought in a man who had been fixing ships since he was young.

He carried a large bag of tools with him and when he arrived immediately went to work. He inspected the engine very carefully, top to bottom.

Two of the ship's owners were there watching this man, hoping he would know what to do. After looking things over, the old man reached into his bag and pulled out a small hammer. He gently tapped something. Instantly, the engine lurched into life. He carefully put his hammer away and the engine was fixed!!!

A week later, the owners received an invoice from the old man for $10,000.

What?! the owners exclaimed. "He hardly did anything!!!".

So they wrote to the man; "Please send us an itemised invoice."

The man sent an invoice that read:

Tapping with a hammer...................... $2.00

Knowing where to tap........................ $9,998.00

Effort is important but experience and knowing where to direct that effort makes all the difference.

Brands known for their simplicity

1. Netflix

Whether you're vegging out at home or aboard a cross-country red-eye, hosting your own personal Bill Murray retrospective or rewatching all 10 seasons of *Friends* is as easy as reaching a device, opening an app, and pressing Play. The platform takes ease of experience one step further, with algorithms that track your viewing patterns, eliminating the arduous decision-making process of what to watch next.

2. ALDI

With 'easy-to-use' stores and 'direct and helpful' information, ALDI understands the real path to its shoppers' hearts is a stress-free, no-frills shopping experience. People credit the German brand for helping them 'save time' as well as its 'reasonable prices.' Simple, consistent floorplans plus uncomplicated offers, high-quality products, and excellent customer service, proves that ALDI is determined to give value back to its loyal customers.

3. Google

While it's a radically different world since its launch 20 years ago, Google hasn't strayed from its original mission. The tech industry may have faced scandals over the past year, but the universally 'accessible' brand soldiers on, pushing the boundaries of available technologies to organize the world's information.

4. YouTube

YouTube's simple, easy-to-navigate interface prevents the inundation of information. And, this year, the video-sharing platform doubled down on this tenet, announcing they would prohibit climate-change-denying advertisements.

5. McDonald's

McDonald's makes simplicity delicious. Take their French fries. The humble potato is sliced, fried, and salted to perfection. Since the onset of the COVID-19 pandemic, McDonald's has added a new ingredient: goodwill. The company has donated millions of meals to first responders, healthcare workers, and educators. Food and philanthropy make for an excellent combo meal.

6. Samsung

Samsung is renowned for their innovation. Take The Frame. The television transitions effortlessly from displaying content when turned on to works of art when turned off—the simple, picture-frame-like trim accentuating the masterpieces.

7. Amazon

Amazon is a revolutionary—from e-commerce to philanthropy and entertainment. Recently, the online marketplace revolutionized another medium: podcasts. Now offering synchronized transcripts of select podcasts for deaf and hard-of-hearing audiences, Amazon simplifies the user experience and advances inclusion and equity ambitions. Yet again, Amazon offers a prime example for delivering curated, hyper-personalized experiences.

8. Uniqlo

In this long period of loungewear, the Japanese retailer Uniqlo has outfitted consumers worldwide. One way the emporium has attracted broad appeal is through their partnerships with such cultural icons as Disney and Sesame Street. In addition to these chic collaborations, Uniqlo's capsule collection includes quality, longevity, and simplicity.

9. Spotify

With more than three million podcasts and 70 million songs, Spotify occupies airwaves worldwide. Recently, the streaming service introduced Car Thing, a dashboard-mounted, voice-activated device that enables users to simply—and safely—navigate through content.

How to Make Something "Simple"

Calling something simple is like calling it beautiful—the specifics can be hard to nail down, and what's simple to one person might be complicated to another.

1. **Get the basics right:** All of these brands deliver on their basic promise. They don't confuse customers with hundreds of combinations of offers; they deliver what customers came for quickly and easily. ALDI gives you a low-cost, low-brand grocery experience—even if they offer caviar once in a while, they do it at bargain-

basement prices without frills, bought from a cardboard box on a metal shelf and the fastest cashiers in the world.

2. **Provide tangible value:** No customer cares if you offer a simple experience but don't provide something they need. Each of these simple brands is a master at building products and services that customers are willing to buy, repurchase, and recommend to their friends.

3. **Keep the experience transparent:** The best of these brands offer something unique. Their simplicity is tied with honesty. They don't confuse with value bundles, rely on random and radical promotions, or hide their pricing. When you subscribe to Netflix, there's no doubt that you'll get exactly what you paid for: a streaming service that just works. They may raise their prices, but they'll never have blackout periods for comedies or charge overages for binging *The Office*. Netflix is upfront about their cost to value trade-off.

Chapter 24

Gratitude as a Virtue

Confession – Most of my life so far, I have been terrible at consistently maintain a sense of gratefulness, it is important to admit virtues one is not good at.

I have been fortunate to have a stable childhood with two elder siblings and parents who were always supporting and inculcated a sense of grounding and daily gratitude for having more than enough healthy food, house to live and impeccable health. Born and raised in New Delhi, India in a lower middle-class family, I have been blessed to have attended a private school education with multiple private tuitions and all required comforts a growing adult need.

We had best house and were the first family to buy a colour television, Video Cassette Player and Invertor (for power cuts which were reasonably common in 1980's) in our neighbourhood and suburb. Since a very young age, I could not help but compare our home and financial situation with my cousins and friends from school and hence was never content. I was almost ashamed of the neighbourhood we lived and did anything possible to hide where we lived from people.

As a student, I was above average and, in this area, I never compared myself with the class toppers and I am comfortable to be judged as a hypocrite.

As I mentioned before, I started working fairly early in my life while completing university. I started working in retail part time whilst studying and completing my computer course specialising in web designing and web development and was making decent money. I was never satisfied though and did not hesitate in changing jobs frequently to earn more.

In early 2001 when BPO's and call centres were mushrooming in India, I joined the industry at a first given opportunity. I was in a web chat and email process initially for an American telecom company from there on, I applied and got selected in a voice process when I realised it pays significantly more and served American customers during night shifts for over eighteen months.

My salary coupled with healthy performance-based incentives was significant for my age and experience but somehow, I was still not content. I had intermittent realisation of gratitude which I could not sustain for a long period of time.

My mother played a crucial role in imbibing a sense of gratitude at every given opportunity. Even today, I can almost hear her say

"Son, we are doing much better than vast majority of people, do not forget to be grateful to god when you prey" or

"Son "we have more than we need, never forget that and be thankful to almighty everyday".

Shamefully but respectively, I would often say something like "If I become grateful to what we have, how will I get motivation to achieve more" and various versions of it but she would never fail to remind me the importance of cultivating an attitude of gratitude. I lost my mom in 2019 unexpectedly and I wish I could tell her now that mom, I am really content and grateful in life and to you for all you did for me.

My father would often repeat that "We should be content and thankful that we have zero debt, and we are fortunate to help people in financial need" but I still failed to build this virtue in myself consistently.

Anyway, I did very well for myself and became the youngest manager, Senior Manager and then rose to become Senior Vice President managing a team of more than 80 people, bought my first house at the age of 23, change few more jobs, made more money and changed cities. I was fortunate to buy another house in Mumbai at the age of 29 in a nice suburb.

Though, I was thankful to how life turned out to be fairly regularly by the age of 32, I still could not resist myself wanting more. When me and my wife decided to leave our high paying jobs and moved permanently to Australia and started our professional life from scratch, life humbled me. From being a Senior Vice President of a large Insurance company, I struggled to get a part time retail job with minimum wage.

It took me 101 days to get my first job in Sydney which was in a car dealership calling customers and record their experience of the last car servicing from the workshop. My target was to make at least 80 customer calls daily.

Life has its own (seemingly hard) ways to inculcate valuable lessons that you most certainly need to learn. Life also keeps repeating these lessons (each subsequent lesson gets harder than the previous one), until learning that lesson is the only choice left.

One of my friends sent me the following story which reminds us on the power of gratitude when life seems hard, and I could not resist sharing:

A blind boy sat on the steps of a building with a hat by his feet. He held up a sign which read, "I am blind, please help."

There were only a few coins in the hat — spare change from folks as they hurried past.

A man was walking by. He took a few coins from his pocket and dropped them into the hat. He then took the sign, turned it around, and wrote some words. Then he put the sign back in the boy's hand so that everyone who walked by would see the new words.

Soon the hat began to fill up. A lot more people were giving money to the blind boy.

That afternoon, the man who had changed the sign returned to see how things were. The boy recognized his footsteps and asked, "Were you the one who changed my sign this morning? What did you write?"

The man said, "I only wrote the truth. I said what you said but in a different way."

I wrote, "Today is a beautiful day, but I cannot see it."

Both signs spoke the truth. But the first sign simply said the boy was blind, while the second sign conveyed to everyone walking by how grateful they should be to see…

Chapter 25

Life Changing Events

It took me a while to understand that life's ups and downs are a part of larger plan destined to create a best version of oneself. Some events and experiences though not pleasant, have a potential to alter you in a way that was implausible to imagine before. I have seen my friends, close family members and I go through these life altering stages, I am not sure if my friends or family member would be comfortable for me to share their experiences, at this stage of my life, However, I am beginning to open those chapters of my own life.

It is with no shame; I am admitting to the fact that I have gone through mental health issues and some scars have taken a toll on me internally and shaken my prior beliefs. The objective of opening up is to encourage everyone specially my son when he grows up to not associate shame or weakness with mental health issues. Times like these shine a light on people who truly care for you.

Losing your parent

It is 9th April 2019 at 2:30 am in Sydney and I receive a call from my nephew from New Delhi, before I could realise whether I am still in my dream or talking this call-in real life, I could hear my sister and my sister-in-law crying inconsolably and informed me that my mother is no more. I wish my words could describe my feelings at that time, I became numb, and my mind could not think clearly, it was mixed with a feeling of absolute denial. It was a soul crushing moment for me, and I am to this day (five years later), I get terrified of receiving a call from that number. I truly wish my nephew changes his phone number, but I have never spoken to him regarding this.

My mom was only 63 years old, otherwise healthy and positive about life except for that fact that she was type 2 diabetic for more than two decades. I take a first available flight to New Delhi and realised that my life would never be the same. I am sure that my wife had a difficult time seeing me almost weep throughout our journey, truth be told, I have still not reconciled to the fact that I would never be able to speak to and see my mom. There was rarely a day in my life that I would not ring her and was comfortable discussing almost anything with her.

I have been living away from my parents for more than a decade and I know of my friends who had to fly back to their family during times like these but at the back my mind, I always thought something like that would never happen to me. Believe me when I say this, once you cremate any of your parent, you are never the same person as you were before, it's one of those feelings which cannot be described in words ever.

I have a large family both from my dad and Mom's side and I do not know how, but I maintained a strong façade in front of everyone during my time in New Delhi. However, when I landed back to Sydney, after a few days, the feeling of losing my mom hit me like rock and It was pretty common for me to weep often just thinking about her. One day while driving to get some grocery, I was listening to a song loudly and suddenly I noticed the tears in my eyes, and I felt miserable to an extent that I had to stop the car mid-way and let myself feel all the emotions without prejudice.

No amount of counselling or reasoning like "we all have to die one day" and hearing people say "your mom is at better place than before" can ever make you feel okay. To this day, it's difficult for me not to choke up when I see her picture or play an old video of her.

As I write these words in my home office, I feel a tinge of those emotions hit me like a brick, and I so wish my son had an opportunity to see and feel his granny once. I will take this complaint against God to my grave one day.

For everyone reading this book, if your parents are still alive, just realise how lucky you are. My only request to you for my sake, go and hug them right now, if that is not practically possible give them a call and express your love and appreciation of them. Your parents will not live forever, and you will never be the same once that soul crushing moment arrives. Back to attitude of gratitude.

You will never regret being kind to your parents for all their idiosyncrasies like not appreciating the latest technology or spending money on themselves etc. But I can tell you one thing for certain you will carry a burden of regret throughout your life for not expressing your feelings and leaving important things unsaid.

Losing your job

I have been fortunate to work for great companies and leaders who have trusted and shaped me to become a leader, I have been thrown into challenging projects and problems during my two decades career so far and I would not change a thing if I had a power to go back.

I have shared my story of starting over from scratch in a new country and my struggles landing my first job again. Fast forward seven years, I am working in a consulting company where fourteen to sixteen hours weekdays are not uncommon, and my latest interstate project means I travel two nights and three days every week. For last seven months, my schedule is as follows:

Monday – Work from client office in Sydney

Tuesday – Take a 5:00 AM flight to Brisbane and work from Client's corporate Office.

Wednesday – Work from Client office Brisbane.

Thursday – Work from client office and take a 7:30 PM flight to Sydney, reach home by 11:00 PM

Friday – Work from Client office in Sydney

Saturday – Catch up on emails, reporting, timesheet etc.

Sunday – Depends on energy left.

This schedule has obviously taken a toll on my physical health and family life and both me and wife realised that it is not sustainable when we decided to have a baby.

It is December 2020 and I have had a few days of mandatory shut down to plan and reflect, I also use this time to send feelers out regarding my desire to change jobs. Fortunately, within a few days, I landed a reasonably well-paying job in a bank known for its employee centricity and decent parental leaves as well. My current manager being understanding enough lets me leave on a good note and relatively quickly without me having to serve a three month notice period as per my employment contract.

I start this new job with enthusiasm, the working hours are reasonable, manager is supportive, and I do not feel a need to work on weekends. About two months later, the teams restructured, and I was asked to lead another significant project with changed reporting lines and my new manager was still to be hired.

I accept a new role and then almost out of habit, raise my hands to take on my manager's responsibility in addition to mine until he or she is hired and onboarded. Initiatives like these have always worked well for me and my additional efforts almost recognised and well renumerated and I had a rare opportunity to learn and grow exponentially as a professional. However, in this case, I would soon realise that I had dug my own grave. Apparently, the culture did not appreciate people shining out and achieving better and quicker results then existing leaders have achieved so far and unknowingly I had made a quite a few enemies in the larger team.

Couple of weeks later, my new manager was hired, and it was announced that she would join in next four weeks and relocate from Hong-Kong. Since it was heights of covid 19 in Sydney, she had to complete her mandatory quarantine and thus worked out of a hotel room initially while I covered for her and made sure our deliverable does not suffer.

Her quarantine is over, and she finally resumes her job in office and I dutifully pass all my knowledge to ensure she is up to speed and ready to hit the ground running. By the grace of God, we fell pregnant by this time, and I was delighted to have made the decision of taking this job due to manageable working hours and stability while still on probation.

As I reach closer to the end of my probation and passed all my knowledge to my new manager, her attitude towards me changed. She would give me feedback like "Someone senior complained about me for the quality of my work" and "One of our General Manager mentioned that I am nonresponsive and do not reply to urgent emails". Initially I take this feedback under my wings but gradually start demanding her to validate her feedback by disclosing the names of people so that I can reflect and learn from this. As expected, she was always cagey about it citing privacy and professional concerns.

I later realised that a senior colleague who was furious about me taking larger responsibilities and performing was her best friend and they both made it their mission to make my life miserable. She starts to micromanage me and demands that I share my official calendar with her online so that she can keep an eye on how and where I spend my time and would monitor who I interact with. When she saw, I am scheduled to meet our General Manager on Wednesday 11:00 am, she insisted that I extend her an invite as well.

By now, this environment was toxic for me, and I start to regret my decision of taking this job. During one of those desperate moments, I decide to connect with my previous manager in consulting to express that I am not enjoying this role. The fact that I left on a good note and had a strong performance record in my last role, I was offered a role back in the consulting company matching my current salary which I happily accepted and joined.

I join back consulting in June 2001 and my son was born on 15th August 2021. I lost my parental leave since I was not a confirmed employee in my newly accepted role back in my previous organisation. As difficult it was to raise our first-born baby without any external support due to lockdowns imposed by Covid-19, it was also one of the most rewarding experiences of our lives. During Covid-19, the projects died down and luckily the job was less demanding than before but gradually the pressure of billable hours crept up.

Time flew by and it is 15th May 2002, it's been more than a month that I had worked on a billable project and when I logged in to work from home, I saw a meeting invite from my manager at 7:45 am. Expecting to hear a news of a new project, I was really looking forward to the meeting. I logged in to the Zoom meeting at 7:43 am with palpable excitement and the first sentence from my manager was something like:

"Due to difficult external circumstances, the organisation has decided to significantly reduce cost and protect the balance sheet and due to this, your current role has been impacted and is no longer available". He also added "please do not take this as a reflection of your performance".

I was dumbstruck to even notice that a human resource lady was also on the Zoom call. She finally makes her presence felt and asks me "your severance package letter has been emailed" and "you will have access to the official laptop, mobile phone and email access until noon if you wish to transfer any personal files" also "I was not allowed to initiate or entertain discussion with any of our clients". She ends her monologue by asking me "do you have any questions", I had not yet gained my intellectual faculties back and said something like "I am not sure what to ask and how to react" but my request is that I am in a process of buying our first home and please clear any verification attempts from the bank to ensure we do not lose our substantial deposit.

Just like that I never had any contact with anyone from the company except for a knock on the door three days later from a courier company representative to collect official laptop and mobile phone with the respective charges.

I almost broke down as the consecutive job experiences took a toll on me all at once and I find myself crippled with additional responsibility of a newly born baby and a large instalment of our newly bought home. To add to my misery, this was the pivotal time where I started losing confidence in my professional abilities and my achievements so far seemed like a distant fluke and a stroke of luck.

I start to aggressively apply for new jobs and connect with recruiters over coffee to prove my candidature with as much enthusiasm as I could muster despite my last two job experiences. Finding a new job gets doubly hard when you are currently out of job, and I was doing my best not to sound and or look desperate in the job market.

I manage to land a great new job with impressive salary, benefits, and an industry leading bonus package. My happiness knew no bounds and I was assured that I have landed a role in Sydney to match my significant experience and track record and I have finally arrived.

I begin the new job leaving the past two experiences behind and believed in the saying "God adds difficult time in your life to help you make the best version of yourself". In my new job, my role was to manage a significant part of a five-year transformational journey spread over Australia, New Zealand and pacific countries and manage a significantly large team and budgets. The new job starts with too good to be true experiences like a supportive and caring manager, exceptional opportunity to make a difference and a transformational project that one gets to be a part of not more than once in your professional life.

Months flew by and by the end of my fourth month in the role, I heard some cryptic messages during meetings to suggest that the company is looking to optimise the balance sheet by reducing cost. Our multiyear project in which management had committed to spend multi hundred million dollars over next four to five years was a massive blow to the operating cost.

By the end of my fifth month in the job, the writing was on the walls and selected employees were let go in no specific order and there was chaos and corridor gossip to suggest that the management has decided not to officially commit to our project from next year onwards. During one of our meetings, my manager gave me decisive hints that I am free to look for other jobs considering the uncertainty we find ourselves in.

For me, it was like a déjà vu moment, and I started having sleepless nights. I constantly blamed myself believing that three successive unstable jobs within a span of two years is no accident but a testament of the fact that I am not fit to sustain in this professional environment. This was precisely the time, I started facing some early mental health challenges like fatigue, irritation, lack of concentration and appetite.

I have given more than its share of importance and worked extra hard in my professional life so far and these experiences put certain things in perspective for me:

1. Your job is just a part of your life.

2. Not all companies or managers will be loyal to you.

3. Management does not think much about the consequences of their decisions on employees.

4. Only hard work does not ensure your long-term success.

5. If possible, explore alternate sources of experience and income.

Your family and mental health are more important than your job and I am much peaceful in my life due to these experiences.

Birth of your child

I am not sure there is any other experience in life that comes close to witnessing a miracle of childbirth… your own child's birth.

I got married at 30 years of age which is late as per my family's preference or history and on top of it, I was very clear that I do not want a child of my own. I was successful in giving myself intellectual arguments justifying my rationale like:

1. There are more people on earth today than our planet was designed for resulting in certain catastrophes.

2. There are too many kids in the world in need of a stable family life and it makes sense to adopt a baby at some stage of our lives.

3. Having a child is a lifelong responsibility and adds no value.

My wife was largely on board with an idea but on and off she did express a need to have our own baby. Time flew by as we moved cities than countries and were busy in settling ourselves and build a successful foundation.

Meanwhile, the pressure from friends and family was immense and it became increasingly hard to ignore the constant advice and pressure for us to start our own family.

In April 2019, I suddenly lost my mom, and that event changed me completely and I was suddenly ready and even eager to have a baby. By the grace of God, on 15th August 2021, our son was born and me and my wife cannot imagine a day without him. It was a single most pleasurable moment for me to witness my son being born and taking care of a new life.

Having a baby is like falling in love all over again.

Arrival of your baby fills a gap in your life that you did not know existed.

Chapter 26

Incidents, Irritations & Delays

It is 26th November 2008 in Mumbai, the date I have been looking forward to for more than a month now. My fiancé' is expected to visit me from New Delhi in the afternoon flight and I am getting ready to pick her up from the airport and show her around before heading back to my apartment. I have been cleaning my apartment since last evening and it is not up to her standards yet but it's almost 11:30 am and I better leave for airport since there is one thing you can never trust about Mumbai city is its unending traffic.

As I board my apartment lift and reach the basement parking, I find a flat tire on my almost new car. Irritated by this incident, I ponder on the two choices:

1. Take a cab or

2. Quickly change the tire and drive as fast as I can.

As I reluctantly chose to change the tire and drive maniacally, my neighbour drives in the basement to park his car. He has met my fiancé' and is aware of my plans to pick her up today, looking at my sweaty face, he kindly offers me to take this car instead and worry about the spare tire later. I reluctantly accept his offer and ask him if he has any plans that I am potentially impacting by taking away his ride, he says I plan to drive to the city to have a few drinks with my colleagues at Café Leopold and need to leave by 5:30 pm. I promise to be back before that time and quickly drive in the direction of western express highway which unfortunately is the only connection to the Airport.

Thankfully I managed to reach the airport on time and fiancé did not have to wait for more than 5 minutes since the flight ended up being on time which is unusual. I excitedly pick her up and we impromptu decide to have a nice Thai lunch at Santacruz and were free by 4:30 pm which was enough time for us to reach home and hand-over the car to my neighbour friend.

As we managed to reach Andheri, there was an unending traffic almost bumper to bumper and we did not move a hundred meters in the last fifteen minutes. I called my neighbour with this development and humbly offered to pay for his taxi ride to and from the city since I inadvertently spoiled his plan. He told me taxi might not work as he was supposed to pick his colleagues along the way, he sounded frustrated and decided to postpone his plan.

I was distraught being responsible and kept thinking about the ways I can make it up to him soon. It was almost 6:00 pm that I managed to reach home and I did not have the courage to face him and handed over the car keys to the security guard instead.

By 7:15 pm, the news was buzzing all over India on the hideous terror attack in Mumbai an extent of which was never experienced before. Eight of the attacks occurred in South Mumbai: at Chhatrapati Shivaji Maharaj Terminus, the Oberoi Trident, the Taj Mahal Palace and Tower hotel, the Leopold Cafe, the Cama Hospital the Nariman House, the Metro Cinema, and in a lane behind the Times of India building and St. Xavier's College. There was also an explosion at Mazagaon, in Mumbai's port area, and in a taxi at Vile Parle. By the early morning of 28 November, all sites except for the Taj Hotel had been secured by the Mumbai Police and security forces. On 29 November, India's National Security Guards (NSG) conducted Operation Black Tornado to flush out the remaining attackers; it culminated in the death of the last remaining attackers at the Taj Hotel and ended the attacks.

My neighbour along with his colleagues had a table booked at the very Leopold Café at 7:00 PM which was an epicentre of the attack and even to this date, one can see the bullets engraved in the walls and it took them years to finally be open for business again.

Needless to say that my neighbour was thankful for me being late, so not all irritations are bad.

One of my pet peeves is a driver in front me driving at 50 kmph in a 60 kmph lane, or some other version of driving slower than the speed limit. I know it sounds crazy and stupid and it almost is, and I have gotten better with more grey hair on my head, but truth be told it still bothers me. Though I prefer not to honk on slow drivers, I make it a point to look them in the eye and show my displeasure when I finally overtake that car…I know its juvenile but who says I am perfect!

One incident like this changed my perspective and the impact of it was spread across other areas of life as well and the incident goes like this…

A car ahead was moving like slower than allowable speed limit for more than 10 kms and not giving me way in spite of my continuous blinking of headlight!

I was on brink of losing my cool and honk when I noticed the small sticker on the car's rear.

It reads…

"Physically challenged; Please be patient."

And that changed everything!! I immediately went calm and slowed down!!

In fact, I got a little protective of the car and the driver.

And then it struck me. Would I have been patient if there was no sticker!?

Why do we need stickers to be patient with people!?

Will we be more patient and kinder with others if people had labels pasted on their foreheads?

I reached work a few minutes late, but it was ok!

Labels like:

- Lost my job.

- Fighting cancer.

- Going through a bad divorce.

- Suffering Emotional abuse.

- Lost a loved one.

- Feeling worthless.

- Financially messed up.

- …and more like these.

Everyone is fighting a battle we have no idea about.

The least we can do is be patient and kind.

We don't have to put people through the pressure of explaining over times before we understand their pains and offer our little best.

As you go through each passing day always remember there's an invisible label on everyone.

A simple virtue of patience may just be the respect you're according that invisible label.

Chapter 27

Illusion of Expertise

No man is a prophet in his own country......Bible

Expert is an ordinary fellow from another town......Mark Twain

Expert is a man fifty miles from home with a briefcase......Will Rogers

I consider myself as spiritual but not religious, I think part of the reason is that I have been brought up in the environment focussed on karma more than prayer. The irony is I have a keen interest in reading about religion and at the time of writing this, I have read the following cover to cover:

- Bhagwat Geeta
- Holy book of Quran Sharif &
- Bible

While I do not profess to any particular religion, I frequently visit temples, churches, synagogues and mosques seeking divine peace and direction, I wander of grave contradictions in religious beliefs and practices.

Over a period of time, I have read significantly about Jesus (a born Jewish) & Christianity and often wander "Why was Jesus not believed and rejoiced in his hometown"? While Jesus was known to restore people to life with his healing touch, the Jewish community did not believe him and accused him of blasphemy.

"He went away from there and came to his hometown, and his disciples followed him. And on the Sabbath, he began to teach in the synagogue, and many who heard him were astonished, saying, 'Where did this man get these things? What is the wisdom given to him? How are such mighty works done by his hands? Is not this the carpenter, the son of Mary and brother of James and Joses and Judas and Simon? And are not his sisters here with us?' And they took offense at him. And Jesus said to them, 'A prophet is not without honor, except in his hometown and among his relatives and in his own household.' And he could do no mighty work there, except that he laid his hands on a few sick people and healed them. And he marvelled because of their unbelief." - Mark 6:1-6

While there are many interpretations of why Jesus was not considered as Messiah in his own town, the Christians believed he was divine and worshipped him religiously all over the world. No wonder, Jesus is believed to have said:

"Only in his hometown, among his relatives and in his own house he is a prophet without honour."

The wisdom of bible is not lost in today's times where experts are believed to be people from outside. Over my career, I have worked with great organisations who have often at the time of a problem or a crisis, decided to trust and hire so called experts from consulting organisations over their own experienced employees. The irony is that the consultants actually understand the potential causes of a problem and their plausible situations from the very same employees that the organisations do not trust in the first place.

Common saying goes as:

"A consultant is someone who borrows your watch to tell you the time." During my time as a consultant, I can affirm that this is 100% true.

In my personal life as well, I have countless examples of seeking advice from friends to validate the suggestions from the family members.

Chapter 28

Eagle and a Mouse

Over a period of my professional life, I have been lucky to have opportunities to attend countless trainings and retreats, some of these included:

1. Leadership Seminar

2. Conflict Management

3. Strategic Direction

4. Change Management

5. Crisis Management &

6. Professional Development

I truly believe that I have learned significantly from these trainings and retreats which have played a crucial role to improve myself professionally and personally, some of course have contributed more than others.

One of the leadership seminars that I attended in the year 2019 was a character-building experience for me, my key take away from that experience was:

"We need to balance the eagle and a mouse within us".

On a freezing day of July 2019 in Melbourne, Australia, a group of twenty mid-level leaders from across the organisation assembled in the River Room of Crown Melbourne Hotel, an iconic venue on Yarra River. I am greeted enthusiastically by Kathy at the concierge where I register myself, she issues me my visitor's pass with a lanyard and two coffee vouchers that can be redeemed at any café in the grand hotel.

It is 8:40 am and I grab an extra hot latte courtesy Kathy and make my way to the river room at level 27 for a session scheduled to start at 9:00 am. I enter a grand door and am pleasantly surprised by the lay out of the room, the training chairs are replaced with comfortable yet stylish mattresses with round pillows. We are instructed to take our shoes off and make ourselves comfortable, I opt for a white mattress at the corner where I can have an uninterrupted view of the Yarra River throughout the day.

Ms Natalie begins the session with a charged up good morning and introduces general principles leadership and the stressful situations that leaders across all levels are exposed to on regular basis. She encourages all of us to share some of the challenges we face as managers or leaders, some of the situations shared by people included:

1. Management does not understand how difficult is to manage and improve the performance of so many different employees in our teams.

2. Team members do not value their counsel and do not wish to take additional responsibilities.

I notice a man in his fifties wearing a white polo t-shirt and blue denims enter the room at around 9:40 am and quietly stands at one corner observing the surroundings and sharp at 10:00 am, he stands in the middle of the room and introduces himself as Steve Raynor.

Steve introduces himself with a couple of jokes to lighten the mood and the way he took charge of the room proved his experience and expertise. He introduces a topic:

"Leadership in unfair, but so is life".

He clicked the remote and the below image appeared on a giant screen in the middle of a wall:

He adds leadership in professional or personal life is no different from a life of an eagle. The mouse on the other hand is content doing menial work, spend time whining and criticizing the situations.

The eagle learns to fly by being pushed out of the nest by mama and initially in its fledgling struggle to survive, frantically flaps it wings, falling in the process, and eventually being saved by mama eagle before it hits the ground. Then the process repeats until the eagle learns to fly.

Once the eagle learns to fly the greater learning begins. On its own, the eagle now must hunt for food. Learning to fly is an important part of the process, but now the eagle must learn to deal with other challenges. For example, with its keen and acute vision the eagle can spot its prey from a great distance. If for example the prey is a mouse, the eagle will upon spotting the mouse begin its descent in an attempt to capture the mouse. However, sometimes the mouse spots the eagle. Just as the eagle wants the mouse so that it can eat it and survive, the mouse does not want to be eaten. So as the eagle moves in the direction of where the mouse is, the mouse may move and go to a spot where the eagle is not headed. Or the winds may shift just a bit and the eagle that has yet to learn to deal with the winds, misses the mouse, having its flight shifted even slightly enough to miss the mouse.

What does the eagle do? It learns. It doesn't whine and complain that life is unfair. It doesn't lobby for rule changes demanding that the winds are forced to comply with its flight, or that mice remain where they are when sought after for food. The eagle has no power to cause that change. The Eagle, in its instinctive, natural knowing, learns and adapts and seeks other opportunities. Eventually the eagle learns to deal with the winds and learns to fine tune its hunting skills. In the process it discovers its greater natural ability to live, grow and thrive.

Over the years of training and coaching thousands of people, I have witnessed over and over the lesson of the eagle being a great tool to assist and support my clients to discover and implement their greater talent. While the eagle doesn't have the luxury of complaining and whining, hoping that something changes things to make life easier for it, as it will die waiting, the human often gets in its own way of discovery of its greater potential and power by substituting the idea of having power over others and attempting to control them as a counterfeit form of discovering their own power.

In life there are others who have different visions and purposes other than our own. In life, the winds may change from time to time and what we once felt was certain and expected can change suddenly. We can whine, complain, demand compliance using guilt, shame, labelling, name calling, stereotyping, edicts and other forms of force. Or we can, like the eagle, learn to deal with the situation, rather than allow the situation to deal with us.

When a door of opportunity closes, the eagle looks for new opportunity, not having the luxury of complaining. It will die in the process. Many individuals, in seeking opportunity, find that some doors are closed. Instead of looking for and creating new opportunity, they seek to demand the closed door opens for them. Living in that world of scarcity rarely, if ever, results in the fulfillment and growth they would seek. It may create a short-term sense of victory, but long term, like the eagle, the discovery of the greater part of that person dies as they learn to rely on force and control, rather than their own merits, to create new opportunities.

The foresight learning is to balance the eagle and the mouse within us. At times we are the mouse, scurrying about the floor, picking up every crumb, scrutinizing everything in our small world.

At other times we need to become like the eagle—to fly over the situation and to assess the bigger picture. From a higher or greater witness viewpoint, we can look down onto the stage of our story and see the bigger picture of what's going on. While seeing our lives from this witness viewpoint, we are less likely to get caught in the little minutia of the moment.

If we can learn to balance the energy of both animals within us, we can bring greater balance into our lives and into the world.

Chapter 29

All Things Money

I make it a point to never enter into an argument with friends and colleagues over three things:

1. Money

2. Religion &

3. Politics

My reasons for not disagreeing with others or not preaching about money are fairly simple:

1. I have read 29 books about money and most authors contradict their own theories.

2. Most people develop their psychology of money during growing up years with influences from family and friends.

3. When you tell people that managing and growing money is simple, they laugh at you.

4. Banking industry, Media and financial planners have built billion dollars fee businesses by complicating finances.

Define your own Rich or wealthy life

I vividly remember my dad telling me and my siblings that his target was to save 100,000 Indian Rupees and then he will happily retire. At the time of writing this, he is 72 years old, healthy and still working in spite of having a net worth of more than 500 times of his initial dream target. The reason I mention this is to emphasis a point that there is no magic financial $ number to define a rich or a wealthy life. The context or personal priorities is important, imagine how would Elon Musk define a rich life? What $ number will a man with a net worth of ~$190 billion USD put on his vision board to be considered Rich or Wealthy?

My wife loves luxury bags, and she plans for them financially and buys them regularly and her usual predicament or a source of stress before going out is to decide which luxury bag to combine with her dress out of her vast collection? 😊. I know she would prefer me to wear designer belts and designer clothes, but she understands and appreciates that this does not motivate me.

I do not think twice before spending on creating experiences and or medical/wellness for my dad, wife and son and I love to buy quality shoes and books and go on vacations. Let me be clear that I do not want you to ditch financial goals, I am just sharing the insights I gained from my family and research. Quintessential example of using hindsight to foresight……

There is no such thing as objective wealth to make one happy, wealth is relative to your expectations.

Morgan Housel says it best "*in Finance, spending less than you make, saving the difference and being patient is perhaps 90% of what you need to know to do well*", but what is taught in college is how to price derivatives and calculate net present value.

Compounding

Compounding is like flossing, everyone understands the benefits of but hardly use it to their advantage…Ankush Ahuja

The most powerful force in the universe is compounding interest…Elbert Einstein

Since compounding is the simplest form of maximising return, less said about it is better, so let me illustrate a practical example which proves starting early and using the power compounding almost always beats timing the market.

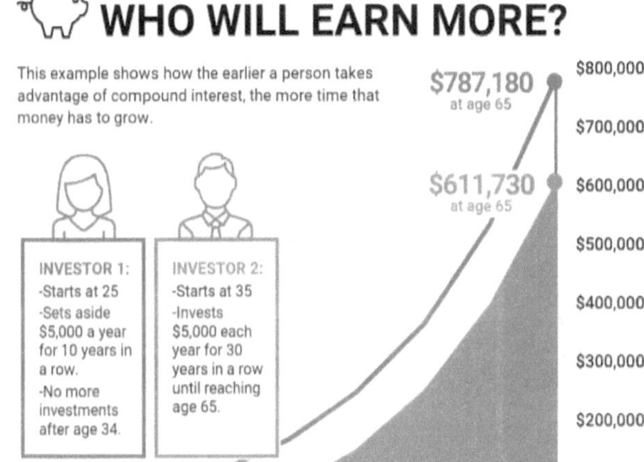

Investing

Wall street is the only place that people ride to in a Rolls Royce to get advice from those who take the subway...... Warren Buffet

The best time to invest was 10 years ago...the next best time is NOW......Anonymous.

During my research, when I spoke to people about investing and probed them precisely to understand the factors that discourage people from it, the common answers I got were:

1. How do I pick up the right stock and who has time to research the market?

2. How do I ensure I time the market to get best returns?

3. I cannot spend hours on a trade platform during my job for day trading.

4. I fear margin calls and what if I cannot cover it?

5. What if I lose my savings?

6. I have missed the last downturn; stock market is overpriced.

Let me suggest a simple, easy and effective way to start without being overwhelmed by financial jargons introduced by the banking industry to create complex products and drive fee revenue and commissions.

1. Open an account with highest deposit interest rate.

    a. This is most likely to be a digital only bank and not one of the big banks in any country.

2. Explore term deposits to park a part of your savings.

    b. This yields the best interest rates for a fixed period. If possible, select auto invest after maturity to use the magic power of compounding.

3. Exchange Traded Funds or Mutual Funds.

    c. In my opinion, ETFs are the simplest and easiest way to get into investment markets because they are low-cost and hold a basket of stocks or other securities, increasing. Diversification allows you to spread your contribution.

Try any combination of the above three and see your investments grow over time. Most of the financial service providers offer and easy digital experience to:

1. Open any of these accounts

2. Make changes to the contribution and frequency.

3. Auto debit

4. Redemption

5. Increase or decrease your contribution.

My last advice is to resist redemptions from these accounts unless there are no alternatives in case you need any emergency access and spend guilt free on things and experiences truly matter to you.

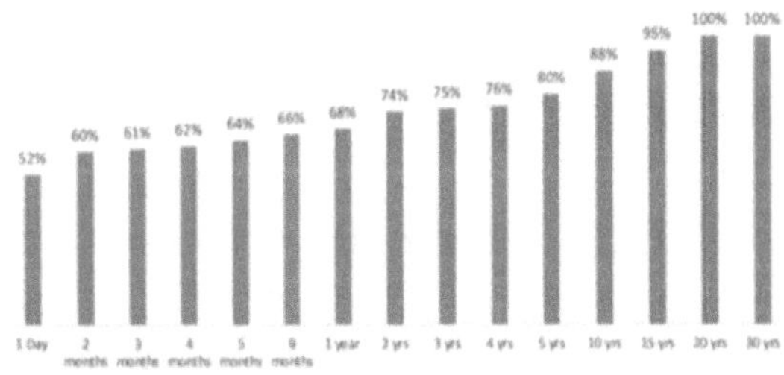

Source: Collaborativefund.com - Morgan Housel.

Budgeting

One of my neighbours and a friend who is incidentally a financial planner and charges $350 an hour teaching goal setting and budgets recommends this budget calculator. Please be mindful, I have intentionally used just 40% of the calculator to prove how complicated and time consuming this unnecessary complexity is:

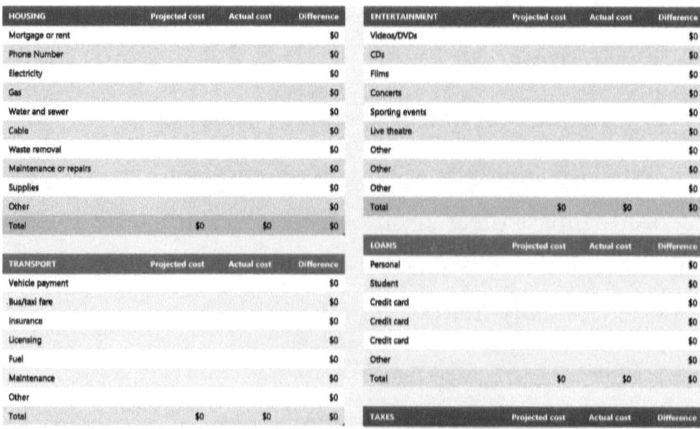

HOUSING	Projected cost	Actual cost	Difference
Mortgage or rent			$0
Phone Number			$0
Electricity			$0
Gas			$0
Water and sewer			$0
Cable			$0
Waste removal			$0
Maintenance or repairs			$0
Supplies			$0
Other			$0
Total	$0	$0	$0

TRANSPORT	Projected cost	Actual cost	Difference
Vehicle payment			$0
Bus/taxi fare			$0
Insurance			$0
Licensing			$0
Fuel			$0
Maintenance			$0
Other			$0
Total	$0	$0	$0

ENTERTAINMENT	Projected cost	Actual cost	Difference
Videos/DVDs			$0
CDs			$0
Films			$0
Concerts			$0
Sporting events			$0
Live theatre			$0
Other			$0
Other			$0
Other			$0
Total	$0	$0	$0

LOANS	Projected cost	Actual cost	Difference
Personal			$0
Student			$0
Credit card			$0
Credit card			$0
Credit card			$0
Other			$0
Total	$0	$0	$0

TAXES	Projected cost	Actual cost	Difference

My philosophy of managing money is simple:

1. I Save + Invest more than half of my income. (mortgage payment is an investment since I am creating an asset)

2. I never buy unnecessary stuff even when it is almost free.

3. Apart from mortgage, I never buy anything on loan.

4. I always buy the best I can afford because cheaper is often more expensive.

5. My spending does not change much depending on my account balance since I spend on stuff that is necessary.

6. I do not sweat about expenses I cannot control like medical treatments.

Let me illustrate the pitfalls of keeping of trying to budget all expenses:

Budgeting creates an idea of scarcity

Budgeting tools are designed to track every dollar you spend and creates unnecessary guilt if you really crave for something like a latte or a nice lunch occasionally and makes you frustrated or bitter. The time spent on keeping a record of every transaction and reconciling at the end of every day, week or a month is a hassle and a headache. Instead of becoming a tool for empowerment by encouraging you to be smart about your money, the budget becomes a source of anxiety and stress. Ugh. Budgets are the worst.

One of my colleagues told me his two problems with expense tracking:

-   When your finances are good, expense tracking provides relatively little value.

-   When your finances are a mess, expense tracking isn't enough to save you.

In my research on budgeting and expense tracking, I have had discussion and feedback from 143 adults so far and majority of them have favoured disciplined spending over penny crunching in spreadsheets.

My favourite quote from a 32-year-old banker was *"me and my partner spent about 60-90 minutes per week on an average in reconciling, calculating and putting all our expenses in correct columns"*.

He further adds, either of us can make $200 to $300 per hour doing freelance work instead and more importantly their combined saving per month has not gone up.

Another couple I met described their anxiety as they were unable to factor in $220 discretionary immunisation for their baby in their monthly budget which is not covered by Medicare or private health insurance.

Conscious Spending

Attitude towards money:

Having had an opportunity to meet various people on the topic of financial management, I am convinced on the fact that our attitude towards finance is shaped by the stories about money we often heard in our childhood. I have had friends from extremely rich families who believe in frugality and from lower middle-class families with extravagant lifestyles.

These early beliefs get either solidified during adult life or get thrashed with people making their personal beliefs about spending, saving or investing and about money in general.

Common beliefs and stories I grew up with up comprised on value of money, ethical earning and saving more than you spend. Let me share a short incident that cultivated a sense of conscious spending in me.

Sometime in the year 1990 when I was barely 8 years old, we were going to attend a wedding in Faridabad – a city in the national capital region of Delhi from our home in south Delhi by bus. We were a group of 8 people, my dad, mum 2 siblings, 3 cousins and myself. We de boarded the bus at the last stop and figured that the wedding venue is approximately 1 kilometre from there – this was before smart phones and goggle maps did not exist of-course.

Since all were dressed for a wedding, we wanted to take a taxi or a tuk-tuk to reach our destination. Since we were 8 people, we needed 2 taxis or tuk-tuk and would have costed 30 Indian rupees. My dad insisted that we walk instead, we all cursed him silently while walking in our party footwear. It took us approximately 15 minutes and once we reached the destination, he handed over Rs 30 to all of us to spend on however we desired.

For me, it was a lesson to spend consciously rather than saving money instead. I have adapted this mindset from early on and during our first year of marriage, me and my wife consciously decided to rent a small one room condo and spend on an extravagant vacation to Europe and Thailand. I will take the memories of that trip to my deathbed one day, but I cannot remember any minor discomfort of living in a tiny apartment while our own two bedroom apartment was being constructed.

Another common money principles I grew up heading is:

"Why pay for something when we can make or do it ourselves".

Now, I have realised that this principle no longer makes sense to me. Let me explain, from the better part of last 8 years, I mowed my lawn myself spending in excess of two hours every fortnight carefully trimming the hedges, removing the weeds and general upkeep of plants. Though I take a great deal of pride in mowing the lawn, part of the reason was to save $150 that a gardener used to charge me for every visit.

Sometime last year I realised that I could make more money and but cannot buy more time and for me writing this book became a passion project. As I write this sentence, a gardener has just finished mowing our lawn and is spraying the turf with anti-weed spray. Though he is efficient and has completed the job in an hour, I have managed to almost complete this chapter and enjoyed my extra hot latte.

So, create your spending habits and spend guilt free on things that are truly impactful for you rather than follow what is trendy. Enjoy a 50-year-old $400 bottle of wine or a business class flight to your dream destination.

Credit cards encourage discretionary and regretful spending

It is common to hear people say that using a credit card is a reason for their out-of-control debt position. Whilst I do not advocate for you to own a credit or not, I will summarise the way I have learned to use credit cards to my advantage.

I have been using credit cards for more than two decades and reconciled the financial benefits I have reaped over the last 5 years:

1. $2980 as cashback

2. 6 Airport Lounge passes with an approximate value of $900.

3. Discount on merchandise $390

4. Exclusive complimentary invites to 3 exclusive events including the recent passes to Taylor Swift concert in Sydney.

I have paid $0 in the last 5 years as annual fees.

It's not the medium of expense that matters, what matters is conscious spending whether its cash, online transfer, debit card or credit card.

My learning is focus on learning to spend and your savings will take care of itself.

Chapter 30

Thinking Without a Box

Corporate trainings can often be an utter waste of time whilst a few programs receive great employee ratings during the feedback session just on the basis that it provided few hours or days outside the office environment and social connect with employees outside the team.

The location of the training program also has a significant weightage on the feedback scores, fancier location almost always gets better scores irrespective of the content or value. However, some training programs leave an indelible impact on your thinking and shape you to think as if there is no box at all to be concerned about. As a side mention, the venue of this particular session was the modest office training room.

This module was focussed on "problem solving" and 24 managers from across the organisation responsible for resolving customer issues were invited to learn new tools and techniques.

It is a massive training room in Mumbai office of financial services organisation and as we enter the room at around 9 am, I saw neatly arranged 4 round tables with 6 chairs each with attendee's name cards carefully placed against each chair.

We all take our respective seats, and the program begins with an introduction and expectations from the program. Within the first hour, we covered the basics topics like:

1. Importance of problem solving

2. Problems as opportunities

3. Complaints as a gift &

4. Lateral Thinking

Next module focussed on a case study that was unusual, we are provided with the following:

1. Problem statement

2. 15 minutes to brainstorm

3. Solution

Case study - 1

An automotive organisation headquartered in United States with operations across the world received a following customer complaint. Please discuss amongst your team and document the steps and your suggested solution with reasons.

To,

General Motors – United States

300 Renaissance Ctr,

Suite L1, Detroit

Michigan

U.S

Subject: why my car is allergic to vanilla ice cream?

Respected Sir,

In our home, we have a normal routine of enjoying an ice cream after dinner almost each night. We generally take turns to decide which flavour ice cream to enjoy tonight. Once the flavour is decided, I drive approximately 2.2 miles with my 2 kids to the store to but it. The problem is every time we buy vanilla ice cream, my new GM car won't start. However, if we buy any other flavour, the car starts just fine and is a delight to drive. Please explain why my car is allergic to vanilla ice cream?

Kind Regards

Frustrated Customer

Alex

As a follow up:

General Motors headquarters asked the customer to carefully document his next four nights of buying ice cream. The first night the family voted for vanilla ice cream, and sure enough, after he bought vanilla from the store and came back to the car, it wouldn't start. The second night, he chose strawberry, and the

car started promptly. The third night, chocolate was the choice and the car started fine. But the fourth night when he ordered vanilla, the car failed to start again.

We all spend the next 15 minutes completely frustrated thinking about the following:

1. What does a case study about a car company on a different side of the globe have in common with our business?

2. How on earth we are supposed to know about the internal workings on a combustible engine?

3. When will this training be over?

4. Will they provide lunch?

5. What time can we get home today?

After about 15 minutes, we are handed over an envelope detailing the steps taken to solve this complex issue which read something like:

GM asked Alex to repeat his ice cream visits but to carefully capture data concerning time of day, type of gas used, outside temperature, time it takes to purchase, drive time back and forth, flavour selected, and whether the car started or not.

Crunching the data provided a clue: It always took Alex less time to buy vanilla than any other flavour. With that additional insight, what's your new working hypothesis about the root cause of the problem?

GM then sent an engineer to the store to investigate further. The engineer studied the store layout, noting that vanilla, being the most popular flavour, was placed in a separate case at the front of the store for quick pick up.

All the other flavours were kept in the back of the store at a different counter where it took considerably longer to get served. It was clear that now the issue was why the car wouldn't start when buying ice cream took less time. Once time became the key variable– not the flavours of ice cream – the solution became apparent: vapor lock.

Before cars had fuel injection, when a car was shut off, it needed time to cool down before it would restart. This happened to his car every night but because Alex got vanilla more quickly, the engine was still too hot for the vapor lock to dissipate. But the extra time needed to get the fancy flavours allowed the engine to cool down sufficiently to start. Problem solved.

Lesson Learned: If your initial interpretation of the solution to a problem doesn't make logical sense, search for alternative solutions. Refine and test your initial hypothesis, dig deeper, get data.

Don't confuse correlation with causation. Just because buying vanilla correlated with a stalled car, that was not the causative factor. The rooster crowing in the morning doesn't cause the sun to rise, though it may like to think it does.

Be strategic and intelligent about discovering root causes. And be assured that your car should start regardless of what ice-cream flavour you are hungry for.

I read the details of the solution and lessons learned more than once and felt like a eureka moment for me. Problem solving is not restricting yourselves for obvious answers but exploring overlooked aspects, challenging norms and looking past apparent boundaries.

In short, thinking without the box.

After an insightful session of deep discussion, it is time for a lunch break and the instructor announces that we have one more case study to discuss and deliberate right after the lunch break. I could not be more excited to resume back.

We resume back, quickly debrief the day so far and everyone is looking forward to the envelopes on our table with material for another case study.

Case study – 2

An owner of the building "Windsor Corporate Towers" which is a 100-year-old has been receiving complaints about the elevator. It is old, slow, and frequently needs maintenance which means it is not available for use for a number of hours. It is not uncommon to witness unending queues during morning, lunch, and an evening rush. Situation has reached a stage prompting number of tenants threatening to cancel their lease if the situation does not improve. It is a heritage building and the builder has long term plans to upgrade the tower in a few years.

PROBLEM FRAMING

"The elevator is too slow."

SOLUTION FINDING →

SOLUTION SPACE

"Make the elevator faster."

Install a new lift

Upgrade the motor

Improve the algorithm

Potential solutions:

1. Replace the lift.

2. Install a strong motor.

3. Upgrade the algorithm that runs the lift.

When the problem is presented and reimagined from the thinking without the box, they came out with a much more elegant solution:

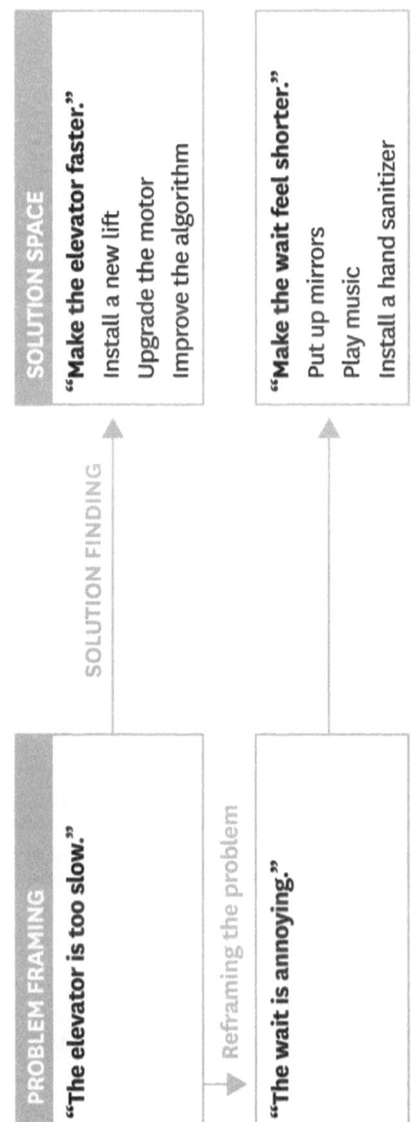
PROBLEM FRAMING
"The elevator is too slow."
Reframing the problem
"The wait is annoying."
SOLUTION FINDING
SOLUTION SPACE
"Make the elevator faster."
Install a new lift
Upgrade the motor
Improve the algorithm
"Make the wait feel shorter."
Put up mirrors
Play music
Install a hand sanitizer

The mirror solution is particularly interesting because in fact it is not a solution to the stated problem: It doesn't make the elevator faster. Instead, it proposes a different understanding of the problem.

Note that the initial framing of the problem is not necessarily wrong. Installing a new lift would probably work. The point of reframing is not to find the "real" problem but, rather, to see if there is a better one to solve. In fact, the very idea that a single root problem exists may be misleading; problems are typically multicausal and can be addressed in many ways. The elevator issue, for example, could be reframed as a peak demand problem—too many people need the lift at the same time—leading to a solution that focuses on spreading out the demand, such as by staggering people's lunch breaks.

Chapter 31

Advantages of being a Little Imperfect

*My only measure of success is how much
time you have to kill…*
Nassim Taleb

The world today screams of perfection in everything we do, the modern-day gadgets like planner, phone and new Apps are helping us get the most out of each and every second of our day. There are Apps to optimise your sleep pattern which suggest the best time to sleep and wake up.

Let's discuss some common areas of life where people are seeking almost absolute perfection:

1. **Finances** – make best use of every cent by allocating money into buckets like expenses, investments and savings ensuring no idle cash.

   Most of my life, I have focussed on ensuring optimal use of money across spending and investment and built models to ensure accurate amount is transferred into different accounts automatically. I learned the hard way when I lost 2 of the most lucrative opportunities to earn significant returns since I did not have enough idle cash to invent:

1. Bitcoin at $9,000 in Sep 2016

2. Tesla stock at $34.29 a share in March 2020

Tesla recorded its historical highs so far $409.97 a share around 2021/22 and bitcoin going north of $73,000 in early 2024. Learning in hindsight is:

Cash can be an inefficient drag during bull market but as valuable as oxygen during a bear market or at a time of a unique opportunity.

2. **Supply chain** – Companies have invested significantly to reach a point of just in time manufacturing to optimize cash flow, working capital and warehouse space.

    In times of today's globalised world, organisations have spent millions of dollars to predict supply and demand to address any potential inefficiencies. One of the global retailers that my company was consulting for reached a level of at demand ordering framework – this refers to a system whereby when a customer picks up an item from the shelf, the backend system auto orders the same from the supplier. This meant items were stocked in the warehouse for no longer than 3 days of expected demand (reducing it from 15 days), this resulted on 7% optimization in warehouse space and reduction in working capital lifting their bottom line.

Then COVID-19 hit, supply chains broke and almost every manufacturer and retailer found itself dreadfully short of what it needed. Empty Aisles and shelfs were a common occurrence across the world leading to drastic reduction in sales numbers. When a little stock did arrive, retailers had to invoke item limits per customers to ensure reasonable distribution of goods among customers.

Things were same for the manufacturing sector where organisations do not stock the parts they need to build products, they instead rely on last minute shipping of components like chips and semiconductors. The irony was not lost when in 2022, during one of the biggest consumer spending times in history, car companies had to shut down production in the factories due to massive shortage of chips and other critical parts. In Australia, the waiting time for an average SUV was upwards of 14 months leading to massive demand of used cars which were selling for more than the drive away price of a brand-new car.

3. **Office hours** – Gadgets and calendars to ensure every second is accounted for productively.

   I regularly encounter my colleagues at work taking a great deal of pride about their packed calendar for weeks with little or no time to enjoy lunch or a coffee break. Seniority or success in today's corporate world is measured by your outlook calendars, the irony is that most of the leaders today have thought jobs but no time in their diary to think.

Chapter 32

Misinformation and Conspiracy Theories

One of the most significant risks in today's world where any and every information is available on a click is rising risk of misinformation. Risk of misinformation ranges from falsely overstating a benefit of a product by the marketers to large scale misinformation being spread to potentially influence an election of the biggest democracy of the world.

University of social media like:

1. Facebook

2. Instagram

3. Twitter/X

4. Google or

5. Youtube

Have a never before power or influence by feeding the information to targeted people curated by big data. The proliferation of social media as an integral part of our day to day lives has given rise to a new paradigm that influences every facet of society, including instant communication and the sharing of or obtaining information across the world. This led to information starting to spread even before its accuracy could be verified, paving the way for the rise of misinformation. Many terms such as, disinformation, fake news and rumours are used interchangeably to refer to incorrect information depending on different factors, such as the format (fake news is typically in a news format), intention (misinformation refers to false information with no intention of harm, whereas disinformation has the intention of deceiving), or the degree of uncertainty about the accuracy of the information (rumours are information with doubt about their accuracy).

Although misinformation is not a recent phenomenon concerns over diffusion of misinformation and harmful consequences have increased recently following events such as the COVID-19 pandemic and Ukraine-Russia war. For example, a widespread false information that drinking highly concentrated alcohol may sanitise the body and kill the COVID 19 virus led to 800 deaths and the inaccurate presentation of the Malaysian Airlines disaster of 2014 as a Ukrainian attack in Russia has contributed to the exacerbation of the Russia-Ukraine conflict.

I have curated a list of largest conspiracy theories we have come across so far:

Covid-19

Probably no event since 9/11 has spawned more conspiratorial thinking than the COVID-19 pandemic. There are conspiracies about the origin of the virus as well as basically every government's reactions. Many people even believe doctors are lying about COVID-related deaths, blaming the virus for deaths with other causes. A distrust of "Big Pharma," fomented for years by "alternative medicine" advocates like Kevin Trudeau (bestselling author of "Natural Cures They Don't Want You To Know About" — a textbook conspiratorial title if there ever was one), have also fed into conspiracies about medical treatment and vaccination.

One of the odder conspiracies mixes long-standing fears of 5G wireless technology with fears about the virus. According to the COVID 5G conspiracy, electromagnetic frequencies from cell phone towers undermine the immune system, making people sick with COVID, researchers reported in 2020 in the journal Media International Australia. Another conspiracy theory claims that the COVID-19 vaccines contain tracking chips that connect to 5G networks so that the government, or possibly billionaire and vaccine philanthropist Bill Gates, can surveille everyone's movements.

As CNBC points out, 5G chips are too large to fit through a vaccine syringe, and even the smallest RFID chips that could fit require a power source that couldn't make the squeeze.

Moon Landing Lie

Every single argument claiming that Nasa faked the Moon landings has been discredited. But even today, more than 50 years later, people discuss conspiracy claims online and on television programmes around the dinner table.

Moon fact: With a powerful amateur telescope, you can see the Apollo landing sites and, if you look at the photos from the Lunar Reconnaissance Orbiter, you can spot the remnants of the Apollo missions yourself.

Were the Moon landings faked?

If you find yourself in a debate questioning whether humankind first stepped on the Moon on 20 July 1969 the chances are that you are woefully underprepared. Most people take it as gospel that the US government, Nasa, the 12 astronauts in total who have walked on the Moon and the 400,000 people involved in the Apollo programme would have neither the will nor the way to fake one of humanity's greatest ever achievements.

But there are those who think the landings were a hoax. They claim the US government faked Apollo 11 and later missions either to deal a crucial blow to the USSR in the Space Race, or to boost Nasa funding or to divert attention away from the Vietnam war. The argument for any of these viewpoint's rests on finding evidence that the landings were faked.

And more often than not, people point out peculiarities in specific images or videos to deal the critical blow. If someone uses these oddities as evidence, what do you say? Here are the most common arguments that support this view, and why each of them is wrong.

Photographic evidence

One of the most popular conspiracy arguments is that there are never any stars in Apollo photos. Free from Earth's light pollution and hazy atmosphere, you would expect to see thousands of stars in all the astronauts' images. Unfortunately, this argument rests on the photos being snapped during the lunar night. All manned missions to the Moon took place in sunny daytime. This meant starlight lost the battle against the very bright surface of the Moon, too dim to show up in photos.

Another common argument is that the crosshairs that appear in many Apollo images sometimes appear to be behind objects in the photos. If the images were real this would be impossible, suggesting someone painted them on. But testing here on Earth has shown that the brightly lit objects make the crosshairs appear fainter. When these images are copied or scanned some of this detail is lost completely, giving the effect that the crosshair is behind the object in certain shots.

Others point to an oddity in a photo of a Moon rock taken during the Apollo 16 mission. There appears to be a C written on it, like a lettered movie prop. Again, analysing the original photo there is no anomaly – the 'C' isn't there. Most likely it was a piece of hair or thread introduced during copying.

A more subtle argument that the landings were faked is based on various misunderstandings of Nasa equipment and lunar physics. A well-known example is the American flag that Neil Armstrong and Buzz Aldrin placed on the Moon. It appears to flutter in the wind in some photos. How could this happen when the Moon has no wind?

In fact, it isn't fluttering at all. A horizontal rod at the top of the pole holds the flag unfurled. This makes it look like the wind is stopping it from hanging down. And there is a fluttering effect because the weak gravity on the Moon is not strong enough to uncrumple the flag. After a little waving while the astronauts planted the flags into the Moon's surface, they have remained still ever since.

Fried by radiation

Perhaps the most convincing argument that the landings were faked has to do with something called the Van Allen belts. These are two giant doughnut-shaped belts surrounding the Earth. They are made of highly energetic charged particles from the solar wind. Some people believe humans couldn't have passed through these belts without being exposed to lethal doses of radiation.

This was a genuine concern before the Apollo missions. And it is the reason scientists behind Apollo 11 made sure they protected the astronauts as best they could. They insulated the spacecraft from radiation with an aluminium shell. And they chose a trajectory from the Earth to the Moon which minimised the amount of time spent in the Van Allen belts.

Readings from the nine Apollo missions that reached the Moon showed the astronauts' average radiation exposure was 0.46 radiation-absorbed dose (rad). This proved Nasa was right to shield the astronauts from radiation. Though it's less than that experienced by some nuclear energy workers, 0.46 rad is around 10 times more than the radiation exposure of medical professionals who routinely work with x-ray and radiotherapy machines.

Proof we walked on the Moon

Of course, until we return to the Moon there will always be anomalies and oddities in the records that can spark new claims that the Moon landings were faked. But it is the sheer size and variety of this record that proves every one of these claims to be false.

From the Apollo Moon missions, there are 8,400 publicly available photos, thousands of hours of video footage, a mountain of scientific data, and full transcripts and audio recordings of all air-to-ground conversations. We even have 382 kilograms of Moon rock that Apollo astronauts brought back to Earth. These rocks have been independently verified as lunar by laboratories around the world, ruling out a US conspiracy.

If this is not enough to convince the most-hardened sceptic, Nasa's Lunar Reconnaissance Orbiter (LRO) might sway them. Today, LRO takes high resolution pictures of the lunar surface from a low orbit. During its mission, it has captured the landing sites and the abandoned descent modules and rovers from the Apollo missions. And its resolution is so good it has picked up the dark squiggly paths that the astronaut's footprints made. Spacecraft from China, India and Japan have also spotted these landing sites, providing further independent verification of the landings.

A final nail in the coffin of the Moon hoax theories is a simple instrument installed 50 years ago by Apollo 11. During their day on the Moon, Armstrong and Aldrin planted a lunar laser ranging retroreflector array on the surface. It's still operational today and allows us to reflect lasers off of it and measure the distance to the Moon down to the centimetre. We simply couldn't do this if we hadn't visited the Moon.

9/11

Eleventh September 2001 changed the world forever in many ways like no other single incident ever in the history of the world starting from the way an ordinary citizen takes a flight to a global fight against terrorist, foreign policy, and geopolitics. Personally, for myself, this was the first time I had heard a word called "terrorism".

Though internet was still relatively new, the first 9/11 conspiracy theories appeared on the online just hours after the attacks, on 11 September 2001, and with the rise of social media, have grown in scope and scale ever since.

Extensive reports by the 9/11 Commission, US government agencies and expert groups have refuted the existence of any hidden conspiracy.

But activist groups in the US and elsewhere, the 9/11 Truth movement, say the facts have been hidden.

Some leading members of the movement have also embraced conspiracies about Covid-19 and vaccines.

And some senior politicians, celebrities and media figures have also disputed the official account.

'World government'

The rise of new conspiracy movements online, such as QAnon, whose followers, among other conspiratorial views, believe a US "deep state" responsible for the attacks, has kept these conspiracy theories in circulation and brought them to a far larger audience.

And online clips from a series of films known as Loose Change have reinforced many of the falsehoods circulating.

Some claim the US government staged the attacks or knew of them in advance and allowed them.

And these falsehoods mesh with more recent online movements' belief global elites plan to curtail civil liberties in response to the attacks and facilitate the establishment of an authoritarian world government.

A claim widely shared online, "Jet fuel cannot melt steel beams," suggests the World Trade Center's Twin Towers were demolished by explosives.

But according to an official report, the crashed planes considerably damaged support columns of both the towers and dislodged fire-proofing.

Additionally, the fires reached up to 1,000C in some areas, causing the steel beams to warp and the eventual collapse of the buildings.

Uncontrolled fires

The collapse of 7 World Trade Center, a 47-storey skyscraper in the vicinity of the Twin Towers, has attracted many conspiracy theories, some of which were trending on major social networks on last year's 9/11 anniversary.

This building - containing offices of the CIA, the Department of Defense, and the Office of Emergency Management - collapsed hours after the Twin Towers without being hit by a plane or directly targeted.

But in 2008, a three-year investigation by the National Institute of Standards and Technology concluded it had collapsed because of intense and uncontrolled fires - lasting for nearly seven hours - started by debris from the fall of the nearby North Tower.

7 World Trade Center was the first tower of its kind to collapse because a fire.

But in 2017, the Plasco tower in the Iranian capital, Tehran, became the second.

Go viral

The fact that the collapse of 7 World Trade Center was announced in a live report by BBC News correspondent Jane Stanley - while it was still visibly standing behind her - has been cited by conspiracy theorists as evidence major media organisations were part of the inside-job plot.

The Reuters news agency had mistakenly reported the collapse of the building, which was also picked up by CNN, just before the live report.

Reuters later issued a correction - but clips of the report continue go viral in the days leading up to 9/11 anniversaries.

Business jet

Some online conspiracy theories suggest US missiles were fired at the Pentagon, as part of a government plot, and the hole left in the building was too small to have been caused by a passenger plane.

But a member of the American Society of Civil Engineers told Popular Mechanics magazine the size and shape of the hole was due to one wing of the Boeing 757 hitting the ground and the other being severed on impact with the building.

Meanwhile, United Airlines Flight 93 crashed near Shanksville, Pennsylvania, after passengers tried to take control of the plane from the hijackers.

Online theories claim it was shot down by a white business jet flying into a nearby airport.

But aviation officials had requested the jet inspect the area, which it did, reporting back evidence of a big hole in the ground with smoke coming out of it.

Vice-President Dick Cheney later revealed in his autobiography that following the attack on the Twin Towers, he had ordered the shooting down of any commercial airliner believed to have been hijacked.

But in the chaos and confusion that followed the attack, his order was not passed to fighter pilots, according to the 9/11 Commission report.

'Jewish elites'

Another theory falsely claims no Jewish people were killed in the attacks because 4,000 Jewish employees at the World Trade Center had received advance notice not to turn up for work.

Believers conclude the Israeli government mounted the attacks to goad the US into attacking its regional enemies or responsibility lies with powerful Jewish elites who control world events from the shadows.

But of the 2,071 victims of 9/11 who worked at the World Trade Center, 119 were confirmed to be Jewish and at least a further 72 were believed to be Jewish.

That would constitute 9.2% of the victims, according to research by BBC documentary Conspiracy Files, broadly in line with the 9.7% of New York's commuting population believed to be Jewish at the time.

And some estimate up to 400 Jewish people might have died that day.

Similar theories surround other states, including Iraq and Iran, but no evidence of their direct involvement has ever been found.

Before we part.....

Life can only be lived with foresight, yet it is understood in hindsight. In other words, our life is made up of future moments, but the meaning of those moments can only truly be known once they're in the past.

We know that we can't change the past. Until someone comes along and invents time-travel. The details, events, and occurrences are permanent fixtures in our history. But our relationship with these events is dynamic. Our associations with past are constantly evolving as we come to understand more parts of it. What once was a heart-breaking, tragic part of our life can become the source of incredible growth and self-awareness that you are truly grateful for.

That's not to discredit what happened to you. If anything, changing what you think about past events is evidence of the importance it played in your life. You often don't know how things are meant to serve you in the moment. Steve Jobs once said that "you can't connect the dots moving forward", which means you must be patient to arrive at the full meaning over time upon reflection.

What's equally important to understand is that you can't *live* in the past. You can't take action in the past. If you continue to put yourself in past situations and reliving past circumstances you're going to repeat history. You're going to be stuck in the story of how your life used to be which prevents you from being present in how life is today (and how it can be.)

When it comes to living a richer, more fulfilling, more gratifying life, we need to play an active role in creating it. That involves us intentionally designing our future through the choices we make. your future is unwritten and it's begging for you to take control of it! But many people are stuck holding onto how things used to be, good or bad.

That's how hindsight and foresight connect. Hindsight gives you the experience and lessons you need to make better choices moving forward. Our past informs our future and helps angle toward the life we want to lead. But without conscious effort around designing the future with foresight, and extracting value from the past through hindsight, we won't be able to make the same forward strides in your life.

We can't live life backwards. A windscreen is bigger than a rear-view mirror because what lies ahead is more important than what's behind us. The past is past and only deserves a fleeting glance from time to time. To remind us of why we are where we are, how far we have come, and what we're doing to make life better. Using hindsight is not living with regret. Rather, it's wisely referencing the outcome of a past incident—the insight—and applying it in the present.

I have often wondered about the insistence that having regret is a bad thing. There are too many things in my life that I regret and wish they had never happened. As hard as I try, I can't wish those incidents or the memory of them away. I carry them like luggage. Necessary luggage. As life goes on, I've gained another suitcase or two. How can you deny carrying an extra bag? But a strange thing happens after learning what caused the regret.

We gain the strength needed to carry the new bag.

When you have had your own experiences, you feel the pain of the world. You're not unaware of the hurt that was inflicted, the harm that was caused by your actions, or someone else towards you. You care when others suffer. You endure people hurting you. It's only through knowing God's love that you become aware of the suffering of the world. Divine love. Loving every person, every country, every nation, every ally, every enemy, every neighbour, every child, every baby, every tree, every plant, every river, every ocean, every animal, fish and bird, every valley, every mountain, and every planet, moon, and sun in the billions of galaxies in the sky.

How can a business partner's betrayal not leave you with the pain of regret?

When one partner falls out of love with the other, isn't there at least one broken heart filled with regret?

A life of alcohol and drugs leaves a trail of destruction—you have no regrets?

You devout your career to an organisation to be pushed out and forgotten is a bad taste for anyone's palate.

Regret is inevitable.

Abandoned studies, crashed and stolen cars, leaving business too soon, staying too long, discounting your worth, selling yourself short, taking on too much, not speaking up when you should, not shutting up when you should, not leaping first, not shipping your work, not asking him or her on that date, not saving for retirement, not being the parent you wished to be, all the things that didn't work out as you planned.

If you love, you feel regret.

I'm not suggesting wallowing in regret. Stomping in the poo until the smell stings your nostrils isn't a good idea. No one benefits from that. But understanding the hurt or pain yourself, allows you to know how horrible it feels. You have suffered and experienced it first-hand. Seeing any injustice inflicted on others, every by yourself, will sadden and hurt you. You will regret it. A healthy analysis of your role and how you will act in future is acknowledging and addressing the regret.

Hindsight has helped me develop the insights that shaped my personality and character. Strangely, only now do I feel equipped with the foresight to use that hindsight and insight effectively.

Acknowledgement

Writing a book is harder than I thought and much more rewarding than I could have ever imagined.

While I have had a privilege of meeting with and learning from extraordinary people across different stages my life, I cannot thank my family enough for being who I am today.

My Dad M.P. Ahuja for inculcating values like simplicity, living within our means, self-respect, power of karma and being genuine.

My Mom Veena Ahuja for keeping us humble, honest and above all teaching us value of gratitude in everyday life. We miss you every day.

For my siter Ashu and brother Deepak for always being there and supporting my every choice and decision, I am sure few of them did not make sense.

My Wife Khushi for being a beacon of light and keeping up with my idiosyncrasies which I acknowledge must be hard.

And my son Neev, you are best gift I have ever received and a true sunshine in my days and joy in my soul.

www.ingramcontent.com/pod-product-compliance
Lightning Source LLC
Chambersburg PA
CBHW021430150726
47989CB00001B/183